S0-AZK-740

"MR. BASEBALL!"

Probably no one in baseball has had a greater excitement quotient than Willie Mays. Mays has contributed more to baseball than his talent, his astonishing statistics, his home run feats, his great throws and catches, his ability to do so many things so very well: more important than all these is the burning vitality and the heart with which he does all these things. In this cool world he brings—and has always brought—a hot passion to the field.

Here is his exciting story, from the days he learned the game as a child in Birmingham, Alabama, to his great successes of recent years, including that fantastic record-breaking 600th home run!

WILLIE MAYS

by ARNOLD HANO

REMBERT E. STOKES/LIBRARY
WILBERFORCE UNIVERSITY
WILBERFORCE. OHIO 45384

TEMPO
BOOKS

GROSSET & DUNLAP • NEW YORK
A NATIONAL GENERAL COMPANY

COPYRIGHT © 1966, 1970 BY ARNOLD HANO
ALL RIGHTS RESERVED
LIBRARY OF CONGRESS CARD CATALOG NUMBER 79-112491
ISBN: 0-448-05337-3
PUBLISHED SIMULTANEOUSLY IN CANADA

TEMPO BOOKS EDITION, 1970
FIRST PRINTING, MARCH, 1970
SECOND PRINTING, FEBRUARY, 1971
THIRD PRINTING, APRIL, 1971
TEMPO BOOKS IS REGISTERED IN THE U.S. PATENT OFFICE

PRINTED IN THE UNITED STATES OF AMERICA

"You know this baseball game of ours comes up from the youth, the only real game, I think, in the world, baseball. You've got to start from way down when you're six or seven years of age. You've got to grow up with it."

BABE RUTH

This book is dedicated to the youth of America and in particular to my daughter, Laurie.

WILLIE MAYS

Chapter One

It was a windy, slightly chilly August afternoon, the sun shining brilliantly out of a hard blue sky, while down below on the grass and dirt of San Francisco's Candlestick Park the Giants and Dodgers were having it out.

The date was August 22, 1965—a Sunday—and if there has been a more bitter baseball game played in my lifetime I do not recall it. Bitterness on the ball field marks these two clubs. For years when the Giants were in Manhattan and the Dodgers in Brooklyn the teams had clawed at one another; their respective fans had snarled at each other. The history of the league is splotched with the feuding of the Giants' McGraw, Terry, Ott, and Durocher, and the Dodgers' Wilbert Robinson, Casey Stengel, Durocher, and Dressen. Now the teams have moved to the sunswept west coast. No longer can you slip a nickel, or a dime, or a fifteen-cent token into a subway slot and ride a few miles from one park to the other. Now 400 miles of Pacific coast separate the teams, and between them lie the rocky hills of Big Sur, the canneries of Monterey, the rich farmlands of the central valley.

The pitchers on this Sunday afternoon were Juan Marichal and Sandy Koufax, the league's two finest pitchers. Sometimes they, especially Marichal, appeared to hurl the bullets not toward the plate but toward the batter. There was an almost frightening quality to the contest. The Dodgers led the league at the moment, but the Giants—and a host of others—hotly challenged close behind.

In the third inning, with Juan Marichal at bat and the Giants trailing 2-0, Koufax let loose a pitch that slithered through catcher John Roseboro's glove and rolled a few feet behind the plate. Roseboro retrieved the baseball and threw it swiftly back to Koufax, the ball whizzing close to Marichal's head. Marichal spun around and shot a hot word or two at Roseboro, who answered in kind. The two men confronted each other and the bubbling anger, the heat of the pennant race, the simmering feud exploded. Marichal axed Roseboro with his bat, split open his skull. Roseboro tried blindly to get at his foe; players spilled out of dugouts. For a moment it looked like riot, mass assault, terrible bloodshed.

One man stopped it all. Willie Mays took John Roseboro's face in his hands and said in a voice that scarcely hid tears, "Oh, John, I'm so sorry. You're hurt." He began to lead Roseboro away. But Dodger trainer Bill Buhler came out and wiped the blood from Roseboro's face, and somehow the sight of the blood, or perhaps the fact that he could see again, triggered a new response from Roseboro. Again he struggled to get at his tormentor, but again Willie Mays interceded, placing his body between the men. Once more he cupped Roseboro's face, spoke soothingly to a man he would oppose on the field eighteen times a season but whom he considered a close friend.

"You're hurt, John," Mays said softly, and he led the injured man away.

Baseball is a game, yes. It is also business. But what it most truly is is disguised combat. For all its gentility, its almost leisurely pace, baseball is violence under wraps. There is nothing wrong with that. Man needs a place to vent his angers other than in direct confrontation with his fellow man. It is controlled anger that directs a fierce baseball swing; that whiplashes a baseball from a pitcher's arm toward the plate; that slams a man's body into second base, stretching a single. The dugouts the men sit in are like caves, and baseball players are not unlike cavemen as they come out of the shadow of the dugout carrying their polished clubs, their sharpened spikes.

Yes, it is a game, and Willie Mays plays it as well as any man has ever played it. It is a business too, and Willie Mays earns more money playing it than any man who has ever lived. And it is violence. Willie Mays knows this too. Later that day he came up to the plate, with two runners on base and the Giants trailing, and in the radio booth Giant announcer Russ Hodges wondered aloud whether Mays might not be somewhat unnerved after the bloodshed.

Willie Mays had been the peacemaker, because he is a decent human being. But he also has been the greatest baseball player of our time, and though he may have been torn apart by the sight of his teammate and his friend in a savage bloody brawl, though he may indeed have been "unnerved," he always has known what his job is. His job has been to play baseball as well as Willie Mays can.

3

As Sandy Koufax released his fastball and sped it toward him at ninety miles an hour, Mays may have been able to clear his mind totally, the way Stan Musial used to do at the plate. Or perhaps he directed all his passions of the moment—disgust, fear, anger, rage, hate—against the baseball. If there have been greater moments in the lives of athletes, I do not know of them. Peacemaker he had been. Brandisher of the warclub now he was. He hit that Koufax fastball over the centerfield fence, and the Giants won by a single run.

Willie Mays has not hit a home run every time he came to bat, nor have the Giants won every time he does hit a home run. It would have been a poetic triumph had the Giants gone on in 1965 to win the pennant inspired by this one moment and this one man. But life is not poetry, nor is it always triumph. We cannot make more of this single dramatic moment than it was. It did not provide the spark that would carry the Giants into the World Series. In 1966, Willie Mays went on to greater glory and new records; on May 4, he hit home run number 512, to break Mel Ott's old National League record; on August 16, he hit number 535, to break Jimmy Foxx's old record, and become the second greatest home-run hitter of all time. In 1969, he belted number 600. If 500 is the Everest of home-run hitters, then 600 is the Moon. Mays reached the Moon in 1969, but again, the Giants finished second.

Still, this is not a book about the Giants or about a particular pennant race. It is the story of Willie Mays. You cannot remove Mays from the Giants, however, or the Giants from most pennant races these years, so the Giants and their seasons are the seasons of Willie Mays. Nor can you talk of baseball these days and years without talking of Willie Mays.

Heroes and superstars are a vanishing breed. In the old days we had Ruth and Cobb and Speaker. Hornsby, Hack Wilson, Gehringer, Goose Goslin, Lefty Grove, Dazzy Vance. Mickey Cochrane, Dizzy Dean, Pepper Martin, Joe DiMaggio. Men of enormous stature, men who dominated the sport and stamped their brand on the game. Today players are as skilled as most stars of the past, but something is lacking. Call it color, call it magic, but you call for it in vain. Except for Willie Mays.

But Mays is not only the greatest player of our time; he is the most individual. In a cool world he brings a hot passion to the field. Mays has contributed much more to baseball than his talent, his astonishing statistics, his homerun feats, his great throws and catches, and his daring sprints on the basepaths. None of us has ever seen a man with greater mercurial talent, a greater excitement quotient. He can do so much so well and so excitingly—hit, run, throw, catch. Watch him on the sidelines before a ballgame tossing a ball back and forth with a teammate, and you see the incredible grace, the flowing strength, the swift and nimble hands. But more important is the latent explosion which colors everything he does.

He lights up the sport, and he lights it up at exactly the moment it most needs lighting. The game has been hurt by the encroachment of television, which makes it so easy to see a game—see it poorly, of course, but at least see it. The game has been hurt by expanded leagues and by franchises that are swapped like bubble-gum cards. The game has been hurt most by the emergence of organization men with cool personalities in place of colorful human beings.

Willie Mays has never been cool. He has always been an individual. Bill Rigney used to say that just watching Willie Mays put on his coat was an exciting moment, the silky way he moved. And if it is exciting to watch Mays put on his coat, it is that much more exciting to see him rip into a baseball or fling up his gloved hand to intercept a high fly.

He is a superstar, yes, but not a superman. Willie Mays cannot outrun Willie Davis or Lou Brock. He cannot outrun Willie Mays of a few seasons back. He sometimes throws to the wrong base. Balls sometimes leak through his legs in the outfield. (When they do, it is worth commenting on. In a game in late September, 1965, the wounded Giants out of the lead and slipping, an enemy baserunner tried to steal second. The Giant catcher threw badly to second and into centerfield. Willie Mays charged the ball, but somehow it hopped over his glove and between his legs, and the runner kept right on going to score. A wag in the press box said, "That Willie Mays! He can beat you *so* many ways!")

He will end up with a lifetime batting average around, but probably not over .310. Ty Cobb hit .367 over a twenty-four-year span. Tris Speaker, who used to be thought the greatest of all defensive centerfielders, averaged .344 for his twenty-two seasons.

Roger Hornsby hit .358. Hank Aaron, playing at the same time as Mays, is outhitting Willie by some five points. There have been greater hitters for average than this great hitter.

I used to think that Mays could not throw a ball as far as some of the great distance throwers of the past, like Myril Hoag, or as far as today's Rocky Colavito. I'm no longer sure. In late August, 1965, Mays picked up a hit at the base of the left-centerfield wall at Forbes Field and fired a 400-foot strike to the plate to nail Willie Stargell as he tried to score from first. The throw was so enormous and so true that nobody quite believed it, neither Stargell who was still fifteen feet from the plate when Tom Haller had the ball waiting, nor announcer Russ Hodges who had expected Mays to fire to the cutoff man who would then relay the ball to the plate, nor the fans. The throw actually was 406 feet!

Nor can he throw with the repetitious accuracy of Joe DiMaggio. It wasn't really a strike he threw to catch Sargell that day in Pittsburgh. The ball bounced once and then came up to Haller eye-high. Over the plate, yes, but a few inches high. Nor can he emulate the rifle-like trajectory of Carl Furillo. These days Ollie Brown, Bob Clemente, and Tony Oliva seem to throw as well as, if not better, than Mays.

Mays does not lead all fielders in average these days. He drops a fly ball once every couple of seasons. He's dropped maybe ten or twelve in his major-league lifetime. Mel Ott, the great Giant outfielder and home-run hitter of my youth, dropped one fly ball in twenty-two years, and that one only after his

7

eyes began to go bad on him, and he had many things to worry him more than fly balls, such as trying to manage the Giants and wave in relief pitchers from his position in right field.

At the plate Mays lunges at balls and on occasion still swings at bad balls. He throws those 400-foot strikes with a peculiar sidearm delivery, somewhat like a second baseman making the simple 4-3 play. DiMaggio ran like a deer, on his toes, stretched out and long striding, and so incredibly graceful he caught your breath and finally stilled all excitement because he made every play look easy. Mays does not glide; he scampers. When he runs the bases, he runs with his head over his shoulder, looking behind him for the ball. As "everybody" knows, this is a cardinal sin in baserunning. Except when Mays does it, or when Jackie Robinson did it before him. Somehow he still gets there, and this cardinal sin enables him to press the opposition. He knows where the ball is; he can round third and go thirty feet beyond the bag, because he knows where the ball is and where the fielders are without having to rely on information that a coach passes on to him. At age 37, in 1968, Mays managed to steal 12 bases.

Mays does not do everything exactly as the book says it ought to be done, but he gets it done, and he gets it done better. The book is for the pallid, the uninspired ballplayer, the man who learns the game by rote. Willie Mays plays it not by rote, but by instinct enhanced by a special craft, a self-taught art.

No ballplayer is as likely to explode at any given moment in any of a half-dozen ways as is Willie

Mays. In that tense opening contest of the 1954 World Series Mays went hitless, and Dusty Rhodes hit a three-run home run that marked the difference between the Giants and Cleveland. Yet it was Mays' making that stupefying catch of Vic Wertz's gigantic fly ball that really won the game, for had he not made the catch, there would have been no opportunity for Rhodes to bat. And though he did not hit safely, his base on balls and steal of second in the tenth inning again made it possible for Rhodes to bat. There are days—not many—when he does not get on the bases at all and days no fly balls are hit his way, yet he manages to dominate the scene. His very presence does it—a latent quality, the lightning before the moment of the thunderclap. To look at Willie Mays is to see movement and to sense energy, even when he is still.

When Bob Gibson throws a fast ball and by mistake gets it out over the plate, shoulder high, right down Willie's power alley, Mays' eyes seem to bug with wonder, with anticipated delight. Can this be true? he seems to be saying. Has Christmas come so early? The corners of his lips lift in a slight smile and he begins his swing. (And what is Bob Gibson thinking at that very moment? He's thinking, so he says, "Oh, oh. I've just gone and got Mike Shannon killed at third." But never fear, Mays does not hit that ball at a defenseless third baseman. Shannon is safe. Mays hits it instead into the left-field seats.)

We can and we will make a pretty good statistical case for Willie Mays, but it is not in the numbers that you find a man's greatness. It is in some inner characteristic. The key word is "natural." It is an intricate computing machine, carefully geared and synchronized, coordinated down to a hair's breadth, a heartbeat. It is this machine that prompts Willie Mays to turn his back seemingly before the bat has cracked, to race to a wall and reach it at the same moment in time and space that a baseball has completed its 420-foot rainbow and settles like a mote of white dust in the big brown pocket of Mays' glove.

You may gather from this gamy beginning that I am not so much a critic as a fan. Score one for you. I like baseball because it is an exciting game, despite attempts by the organization men to squelch its appeal. I like Willie Mays because he is off by himself as the most exciting of all ballplayers. I am not blind to the crass qualities of baseball. I concede that the prime mover of all professional athletes is money, that some baseball owners are viciously unprincipled men of greed, that baseball is a business. I know, too, that ballplayers are often ill-tempered, foul-mouthed, illiterate men, far below the pedestaled heroes we wistfully make them. And I know that my passion for the sport and my enthusiasm for Willie Mays verge on the immature, that my clenched fists, my hoarse cries attest to a vicarious thrill-seeking.

Still, exciting is the word for baseball. You never really know when it will blow the lid off and turn itself about. The excitement of baseball is never predictable. Its climax may occur anywhere, and even when it occurs, unless it is in the bottom of the ninth inning, you may not even know that it has occurred. For a game's turning point may be a pitch to the first batter, a fly ball in the third, a sacrifice bunt that fails in the sixth, a stolen base in the eighth—and we never know for sure there won't be a home run in the ninth. The whole 1965 pennant race may have pivoted on a successful bunt by Maury Wills in the first inning of that same game of August 22. The bunt seemed to invigorate the Dodgers, to anger Marichal. Angered, he seemed to throw *at* Wills later and at Ron Fairly. Angered and trailing, he exploded when John Roseboro threw a ball back to the mound and came close to nicking Marichal's ear. Next, the wielding of the bat, then the suspension, the missing of three pitching turns, the indifferent pitching on other occasions after he returned, and the Giants losing by a whisker. All this may have turned on a base-hit bunt by Maury Wills.

Such is the unpredictability of baseball. Such is the excitement of Willie Mays. He may turn a game upside down with his bat, glove, arm, legs. And even though we know by now that Mays has all these talents, all these vehicles at his disposal, he continues to amaze and confound us.

There was that startling moment in the 1960 All-Star game at Yankee Stadium in New York. That moment brought into sharp focus the years'-long controversy over which was the greater ballplayer, Mays or Mickey Mantle. Mays, as you recall, had three hits in that ball game, just as he had three hits in the earlier All-Star game that week, and he had stolen a base after announcing to Yogi Berra that he was going to steal a base. It was one of those hits in the second contest that stands out, Mays' drilling a

11

ground ball over second base and into centerfield. When Mickey Mantle loped in for the ball (and you cannot blame Mantle—a crippled athlete playing a game that means nothing in the standings), Mays suddenly exploded for second, beating Mantle's abashed throw. It was a stunning, embarrassing tableau in an American League park, this stealing a base from an outfielder with a strong arm, and if that jury was still out, it came trotting in then and there with its verdict: Mays.

I remember seeing DiMaggio hit a ground ball past the shortstop in an unimportant game one afternoon many years ago and similarly stride for second base, beating the outfielder's unnerved throw, turning a single into a double. But when DiMaggio pulled it off, so sure and graceful, the fans were silent. DiMaggio stilled excitement, except among the true connoisseurs.

When Mays streaked for second, did the fans sit back and say that the employee with the number 24 on his back is certainly worth his weight with the National Exhibition Company; Horace Stoneham's stock surely will go up? Of course not. They stood and roared their astonished pleasure.

In the spring of 1961, during pre-season training, a group of baseball writers sat atop the Hotel Adams sunroof in Phoenix telling lies and dallying with long, frosted drinks, when a young man named Mike McCormick walked by. McCormick was then a Giant pitcher, all of twenty-two years old. Eying the reporters, he said knowingly, mockingly, "You men sure lead a tough life. And all of it on your expense accounts, too." McCormick knew all about easy lives and money; he got something like $55,000 from the Giants—at the tender age of sixteen or thereabouts— even though he had never thrown a pitch in a professional ball game.

Money has become the warp and woof of ballplayers' flannel and of the life around them. It touches all players. A couple of springs ago I interviewed Willie Mays for an article about his feelings of the moment. "How much will the magazine pay for my cooperation?" Mays wanted to know. The magazine would not pay anything, he was told. Mays declined to be interviewed. For a brief spell ballplayers went through the motions of two All-Star games, instead of one, because their pension fund burgeoned more rapidly. The knock is not at Mike McCormick or at Willie Mays or at any ballplayer. They have joined the human race.

But despite this, baseball can be exciting. If you think it can't, go to the ball field and smell the smells of wood and sweat and grass; speak the delicate patois: "All right, Don boy, stick it in his ear." And: "Chop off his leg, Willie." Baseball, in the flesh, is the most exciting game in the world, and Willie Mays, in the flesh is the most exciting ballplayer—a man who seems interested in catching a ball for the sake of catching it more than for the sake of earning his pay. He may decline to be interviewed—after all, it's *his* private life—but he does not decline to put out on a ball diamond.

Mays' dedication to the game does not make him totally unique. Peter Reiser had the same seeming singlemindness of purpose. But where Reiser would, and did, run through the wall half-killing himself and cutting short his career, Mays would make the play and miss the wall. Not always, of course. There have been days in recent seasons when Mays crashed into fences with the best of them. In Philadelphia in September, 1964, making one of the great catches of his career, he crashed into the fence with a terrifying impact, lay still for a moment, flat on his back, then leaped to his feet and tossed the ball to rightfielder Jim Hart. The Philadelphia crowd held its breath, then let loose a roar that continued for five minutes. In Candlestick Park early in 1965, he turned his back on a drive hit by Don Drysdale, leaped for the ball with an outstretched glove, and collided violently, face first, with the wall just as the ball struck his fingers. Naturally the ball was shaken loose. For a moment it seemed more had been shaken loose, but Mays climbed back up, groggily, and Drysdale had a triple. He also had an awesome respect for what he had seen. "That," said Drysdale, "has got to be the greatest effort by a ballplayer I've ever seen."

Other men might ease up on a play like that, let it carom off the wall, or even clear the wall for a home run. Not Mays. He has a marvelous instinct for brushing disaster sidewise, not full-on; he has a knack of avoiding walls and spikes and pitched balls at his skull. But when he must choose between the direct collision or letting a ball fall in safely, he disregards safety.

Peter Reiser seemed bent on destroying himself. Ty Cobb made each game a war. With Mays the excitement is lighter, more exuberant. When a pitcher knocked Cobb down in the old days, he knew that Cobb would get up snarling abuse, ready to run up and over the pitcher's back, given an eighth of a chance. And they stopped knocking Cobb down. When Don Drysdale, or anyone, knocks Mays down, Mays gets up with a defensive grin that seems to say: "You don't watch out, you might even hit me some day." During an exhibition game years ago, Dick Drott of the Cubs knocked Mays down twice. Mays got up the second time and piped. "Hey, remember me? This is your friend, Willie Mays." And where they stopped knocking Cobb down, they keep aiming at Mays. Why not?

So even if Mays does play for money, he is clearly involved with the game for the sake of the game. Not that there hasn't been a change in his attitude toward baseball since that first time he stepped into a major league batter's box on May 25, 1951.

When Willie was a little boy in the steel-mill suburbs of Birmingham, Alabama, he used to accompany his father, William Howard Mays, on short road trips with the United Steelworkers (CIO) semi-pro club, on which the elder Mays was lead-off man and centerfielder. One day the boy discovered that his father got paid for playing ball.

"That seemed to me," recalls Willie, "just about the nicest idea anyone ever thought up."

And when Mays arrived in Philadelphia on that May evening in 1951 to don his first major-league uniform, he said,

"It was like driving through a beautiful park and getting paid for it."

If there is a date on which it became stunningly apparent to me that for Willie Mays play-for-pay had replaced play-for-playing's sake, it was the night of August 28, 1959.

The Giants were a bedraggled crew that Friday night, pulling their once-imposing, now-dwindled league lead into O'Malley's cow pasture—the Los Angeles Coliseum—to play the Dodgers. The day before, they had dropped a doubleheader to the Phillies, then scarcely a National League power. Friday night, before 66,068 spectators, Mays drove in three runs with a double and a home run off Don Drysdale (and wasted a single off a reliefer), made one catch of a ball Wally Moon hit into the murk of left-centerfield that logically should not have been caught, and came in on a sinking line drive by Ron Fairly with a man on second. Mays trapped it so neatly that the baserunner had trouble getting to third.

Dodger announcer Vin Scully asked Mays whether he still felt as he used to feel, that baseball was a game, to be enjoyed as other men enjoy sailing a boat on Sunday, or had it become, as Scully put it, more of a business now? In the good old days, listeners would have heard Mays laugh his bubbling high laugh and say, "Heck, Vin, it's still just a game and I love it." Instead he said soberly, "It's a business, Vin."

No longer does Willie Mays hustle up a stickball game at the north edge of Harlem. The boys of 1951 became the man in 1965 who was touring Job Corps camps and soberly urging youngsters to finish their education and train properly for a profession. And he tackled this tour so energetically—exactly as he plays ball—that one December night he collapsed just before going on stage at a Salt Lake City theatre.

Nature Boy and Natural Man have been buried. But does all this make Mays' play any less exciting? Does it mean that Mays creates no new excitement when he dances off first base taunting Bob Gibson or Jim Maloney, until a ball is thrown away and Mays goes hurtling down the baselines?

Baseball is the way Willie Mays works and lives. It enables him to buy the car he wants to drive, the clothes he feels most comfortable in, the new $165,000 home in Atherton, Calif., thirty-five miles below San Francisco. But within this business, Mays' play still has its old effervescence.

Of all the great time-tempered athletes who have played baseball, it is likely that not one has so excited his audience as has Willie Mays. Ruth gripped you only when he batted; Cobb, truly, only when he ran. Mays grips you when he bats and runs and throws and catches, and when he simply steps out onto a ballfield. This may be the difference between Mays and the others. He is more alive, all the time, than any other player in the business, game, and war called baseball.

Chapter Two

An All-Star ball game is about as exciting as a Mr. America contest. Ballplayers are put in a showcase, paraded before their fans. I've seen more enthusiasm over homegrown rhubarb at the county fair. Quantity is nearly as important as quality. The more great players crammed into a single boxscore, the happier everybody is, except those who bet on the losing team and go around grousing: "We'd of won if that bonehead of a manager hadn't took out Robinson in the t'oid." That Robinson was suffering from a lame back makes little difference, nor does the fact that his replacement hit a three-run home run.

In exhibition ball, the show is the thing. There isn't even as much got-to-win pressure as in an ordinary game in August between two second-division clubs. But there is a subtle pressure in All-Star games, a pressure that slyly works on most ballplayers who don't want to look like bums in front of so many people in the flesh and so many millions more on television and alongside so many stars. On occasion the result has been surpassing performances. I remember sitting in the right-field bleachers of Yankee Stadium in 1939 and watching Bob Feller throw baseballs for three-plus innings (he came in in relief, finished up an inning, and was permitted to go three more full innings), and I do not think I ever saw anybody throw faster in my life. I saw Sandy Koufax more than twenty years later pitch his first no-hitter, against the Mets, and I saw Jim Maloney on the last game Stan Musial played in the major leagues, and it would be hard to say that Feller was any faster than these two young flamethrowers. But he seemed just as fast. Had Feller been throwing those tranquilizing pills in the nighttime, in one of the not too well-lit parks, it would have been necessary to call the cops.

Even more notable was Carl Hubbell's feat in the 1934 All-Star game, fortuitously in New York as if planned that way so that Hub might answer forever those experts who used to carp at the invitingly close Polo Grounds outfield fences. Hubbell struck out Ruth, Gehrig, Foxx, Simmons, and Cronin in succession; when you don't let a man hit the ball it doesn't matter how close the fences are.

There have been great performances by individual stars in All-Star competition and equally distressing ones by the same personnel. In the history of the silly spectacle no player has so consistently put on shows of top billing as has Willie Mays. He has made more hits than any other All-Star performer; he has scored more runs. Mays was the first performer to hit two triples in overall All-Star play; now he is the only performer to have hit three triples.

In the 1965 All-Star game played at Minnesota's County Stadium Willie Mays batted first. It seemed an odd way to treat the game's greatest slugger and home-run hitter, having him bat first, with nobody on base, but Gene Mauch had a true Hobson's Choice. All his hitters, with the exception of slight Maury Wills, were great sluggers. And this wasn't a pennant contest; it was an exhibition. Why not do some exhibiting? Why not have Willie Mays bat first?

Mays stepped in, looked over Milt Pappas's first pitch, then belted the second pitch over the centerfield wall for a home run. Later he ran wild on the bases (with a lame leg) and scored the game's last run as well, and the National League won by a single run. He also made a batch of catches in this strange new park, once falling to his knee and getting up to one-hand the ball high overhead. It was, as somebody later said, a typical Mays performance. Among the All-Stars he is the most All-Star.

In the 1968 All-Star game, again batting first, Mays beat out a dinky infield single, and then when pitcher Luis Tiant threw over to first, trying to pick off Mays, the ball got away from first baseman Harmon Killebrew. Mays trotted to second. Tiant, now totally unnerved, wild-pitched Mays to third, and a moment later, while the American leaguers were pulling off a double-play, Mays scored. The final score: 1-0. Mays was voted the game's most valuable player.

In fact, he is one of those people who have become legends in their own time. Nearly every long-time fan of baseball has his favorite Willie Mays catch, his favorite Willie Mays anecdote, or his truest memory of a base-running feat that turned a game upside down. His most abiding recollection of a Mays home run that cleared all fences and in fact has not yet come down.

In March, 1954, when the Giant publicity drum-bangers were starting to roll out the impending arrival of Willie Mays at the Giant spring training camp after his discharge from 21 months and 108 ball games of Army service, one disgruntled writer in a moment of cynicism sent the following dispatch to his paper:

"Willie Mays is ten feet nine inches tall. He can jump 15 feet straight up. He's a step faster than any line drive ever hit. Willie hits balls that even Willie can't catch."

But with Mays the facts are always more interesting than the myths, and the statistical case for Mays's greatness is a file longer than a tape-measure blast. The publicity drums rolled, Mays stepped off an airplane, Leo Durocher hugged him and said, "This is the key to our pennant chances," and in his first appearance at the plate Willie hit a home run over the centerfield fence. Then he went out to the field, where he made two incredible catches, and panted at the end of the day, "Man, I got to learn this game all over again."

Bill Veeck, as in heck, was the owner of the Cleveland Indians back in those days and after a quick look at Mays reflected on the myth:

"Last year, the Giants blamed so many things on Mays' absence, including rain or an error by the second baseman, that I had to wonder whether one man could possibly mean that much. From what I've seen this past week, Mays means that much."

Still, that was all exhibition stuff. A friend of mine, Dick Kaplan, an editor at *Ladies Home Journal* magazine and that most schizoid of fans, a Yankee fan *and* a Met fan, wanted to bet me before the 1954 season that Mays wouldn't hit .270. Naturally I showed my true colors. I refused.

It doesn't count what goes on in exhibition games in March and early April; the facts of a ballplayer's life begin in mid-April and end in early Fall. So that season, on Opening Day, with Dick Kaplan sitting right next to me in the upper left-field stands at the Polo Grounds (an excellent seat; only half the view was obstructed), Willie Mays hit a home-run off Brooklyn pitcher Carl Erskine. The Giants had won their first real game of 1954 by a single run, the pennant rush was on, and Mays went on to his 75 points more than .270.

During that season the New York *Daily Mirror* used to run a small box about the daily doings of Mays and Duke Snider, also enjoying a phenomenal season. One day in mid-July the *Mirror* box on Mays read:

"Willie Mays made his normal contribution to the Giants Wednesday night. Mays belted his 28th homer and a single, walked once, hit a sacrifice fly, scored twice, and batted in three runs—normal for Willie, but outstanding for others."

Perhaps the most fascinating myth-like detailing of Mays' derring-do is a story told by writer Charles Einstein, and one which Charlie has sworn to on a stack of *Sporting News*. On July 27, 1954, in a game the Giants lost to St. Louis and Harvey Haddix, 7-4, Mays hit a ball into the upper deck in the Polo Grounds, out beyond the bullpen in left-centerfield.

At the base of the fence was a marker, 440. Mays buried his ball a couple of dozen rows back and 50 feet above the fence. Astonishingly (and now the myth begins) Mays hit his home run off a change-up. Five years later at Forbes Field, Harvey Haddix faced Mays in the top of the ninth, the Pirates leading by a run and a Giant runner on base. It had been a long hot day for Haddix; not trusting his fast ball any longer and knowing his curve was starting to hang, he decided to risk another change-up—the first change-up Haddix had thrown to Mays in the intervening five years. As can be expected in such stories, Mays hit the ball over the fence, and Haddix had lost himself a ball game.

A month later the Pirates made one of their visits to San Francisco, and fate arranged matters neatly once again: Haddix on the mound, Mays at the plate, score tied, ninth inning, nobody on, two men out, and the wind blowing like fury toward left field. Haddix took one look at Mays and called his catcher to the mound.

"I want to walk this guy," Haddix said.

"You can't," the catcher said. "You ain't allowed to. That's putting the winning run on, and there are national security regulations against that sort of thing. You can't do it."

"*You* can't," Haddix said. "*I* can. I want to walk him."

"Can't."

"Can."

At this point manager Danny Murtaugh, wondering if his pitcher's arm had stiffened up on him or if

Haddix was more tired than he had seemed, waddled over to eavesdrop. Haddix explained the situation to Murtaugh, who demurred. Haddix pointed to Mays.

"Look at him. Just look at him."

Murtaugh looked and saw a baseball player leaning on his bat. Haddix saw a man ten feet nine inches tall.

"I can't get him out," Haddix said. I know it. He knows it. So let me walk him."

Murtaugh said, "You walk him, and he steals second, and we're in bad trouble."

"He won't steal second," Haddix said firmly. "I'll fix him to the bag with my steely-eyed stare; I'll keep him there with my wily left-handed delivery. I'll even forget about taking the one-second pause before pitching. He won't steal on me." Murtaugh reluctantly consented.

Meanwhile, back in the Giant dugout, then-manager Bill Rigney hastily called Orlando Cepeda over and said, "Don't swing until he's on second. Understand?" Cepeda said, "Me *capeesh*." On the second pitch Mays stole second, and on the third pitch Cepeda singled to left, and the Giants had won another ball game, and Harvey Haddix probably wanted to jump off the Golden Gate bridge.

Myth and fact intertwined, until George Jessel was once quoted: It's possible at this rate that even Willie Mays will be forgotten in 2,000 years." When he is forgotten, and all that is left are the statistics, this is what they will say: Willie Mays is an eighth of an inch shorter than five feet 11 inches tall. It's tall enough.

Mays is the only active ballplayer to have hit 20 or more home runs (35), triples (20), and doubles (26), in one season. He pulled off this feat in 1957. That same year Mays also stole 39 bases, to lead the league. This would have been only the second time in the history of the game any player had hit more than 30 home runs and stolen more than 30 bases in one season—except Mays had hit 36 home runs and had stolen 40 bases the year before. Among active players, only Henry Aaron (in 1963) and Mays' young teammate, Bobby Bonds (in 1969), have this 30-30 record in home runs and steals in a single season. Mays has done it twice.

As a matter of fact, to bring Mays back to the field slightly, only five players have ever hit 25 home runs and stolen 25 bases in the same year. Ken Williams of the St. Louis Browns did it in 1922, Orlando Cepeda in 1959, Aaron, as noted, in 1963, and Bonds in 1969. Willie Mays did it *five years running*.

Mays' 52 home runs make him the Giant's leading home-run producer for a single season, breaking the old mark of 51, held by Johnny Mize and by Mays himself.

Mays used to hold the Giant record for most extra-base hits in a single season at 87 in 1954, his first full major-league season. This mark of 87 exceeds Mel Ott's old record of 81, and Ott was a thunderous hitter. But now Mays has gone beyond both Ott's old mark (on three separate occasions) and beyond his own 87. In 1962, the year the Giants won the pennant, Mays had 36 doubles, 5 triples, and 49 home runs, for 90 extra-base hits.

Mays has led his league in home runs four times, in 1955, 1962, 1964, and 1965. Three of those years he led both leagues. In the years 1961 through 1965 he has hit 226 home runs. In 1965 Mays became the fifth player in baseball history to exceed 500 home runs. In 1969, Mays became the second player to hit 600 home runs. Only Babe Ruth's mark of 714 home runs seems to stand beyond him.

In a single game in 1960 Willie Mays hit three triples. Nobody has ever hit more. In a single game in 1961 Willie Mays hit four home runs. Nobody has ever hit more. That same year he also hit three home runs in a single game and on several occasions two home runs in a single game. No man in the history of the game has ever put together a four home-run game, a three home-run game, and a two home-run game in one season.

Mays appeared in his 2,500th game in 1965. Only Mel Ott, with 2,730, has played more games as a Giant. In fact, on a club whose history bristles with many of the greatest names the game has ever known, Mays is near the top in every offensive category. Within a very few years, if all goes well and Mays continues to play ball at a pace reasonably close to his current one, he will pass Mel Ott in each category and become truly the greatest offensive weapon the Giants have known since Jim Mutrie gazed at the players he owned before the turn of the century and said, "Look at my Giants!" A name was born that day in the 1880's. Today the greatest Giant of them all has come along.

When Mays hit his 51 home runs in 1958, he became the seventh man in baseball to have hit 50 or more home runs in a single year. (The next year, Mickey Mantle, with 52, joined the select crowd of brutes, and now we also have Roger Maris and his staggering 61.)

When Mays hit 17 home runs in August, 1965, he broke a National League record for most homers in one month. Sitting in the stands of Shea Stadium that day late in August was Ralph Kiner, who had once hit 16 home runs in a single month. It has become standard operating procedure for the man whose record has just been broken to take a philosophical stand. To wit: "Records are made to be broken. I'm awfully glad Willie did it. Frankly, it's a relief." Or words to that effect. Naturally Kiner was asked how he felt when Mays broke his record. "I don't like it a bit," he said with disarming candor. *That* is a record not likely to be broken.

And yet this emphasis of the offensive nature of Willie Mays distorts his true value. For all his hitting, and he is among the four or five greatest hitters the game has ever known, Mays' defensive genius is actually the more glittering facet. There are some authorities whose memories go back to the turn of the century and who believe Mays to be the finest of all defensive outfielders. So the greatest fusion of power and speed in all baseball history is also welded to Mays' magic glove and tremendous arm, and the appropriateness of casting Willie Mays as the best of all baseball players, living or dead, active or retired, becomes less outrageous.

But you can also make out a numbers game for

Willie Mays that turns him into something less than awesome. In his three World Series years, 1951, 1954, and 1962, Mays went 15 for 64, for a batting mark of .234. Of his fifteen hits twelve were singles, three doubles. You can generate more power by sneezing. In a single game in the 1951 Series Mays grounded into three double plays. This too is a record. He has yet to hit a home run in World Series play. At his usual home-run pace he should have something like 4 or 5 home runs in those 64 at-bats.

Yet figures lie. World Series feats are nearly as worthless a guide to assessing a ballplayer as are All-Star games. Ty Cobb, in three World Series totalling 17 games, batted .262, 105 points below his lifetime regular season average. Christy Mathewson and Walter Johnson lost as many World Series games as they won. Back in 1903 Honus Wagner made six errors in an eight-game Series during which he also hit .214.

Mays just once led his league in hitting. Stan Musial led the league seven times. Tommy Davis led it twice in a row; so did Bob Clemente, three times in five years. If it is true, as it probably is, that lefthanded hitters have some sort of natural advantage in that they face more righthanded pitchers, it should be pointed out that Rogers Hornsby led the National League six years in succession. And when we think of Mays' 90 extra-base hits as a big figure, Hornsby had 102 back in 1922, also to celebrate my birth, while fashioning a flossy .401 batting average and knocking in 152 runs. In a five-year stretch from 1921 to 1925 Hornsby's *lowest* average was .384, the five year average .402. Hornsby was also the only ballplayer to play

28

for one team (the Giants) while owning stock in another (the Cardinals).

Figures alone, then, cannot make out Willie Mays to be the ballplayer he is. All they prove is that Mays is not the consistent hitter that Cobb was, nor the slugger Ruth was, nor the base-stealer Maury Wills is, nor the businessman Hornsby was. But figures also prove—what we set out to prove—his astonishing versatility, his greatness in so many ways.

By the end of 1965 he'd become the second greatest home-run hitter in his league's history. The next year he became the second greatest home-run hitter in the history of both leagues, and the greatest righthanded home-run hitter of all time. He trailed only Babe Ruth. Of course, Mays is a better runner, a better fielder, a better thrower than Ruth (who was far better than average in each of these categories). And though it may be said that today's stars lack the color of past stars, nobody suggests today's players are not as talented. If I may go further, I think today's players are the best ever to perform on a ballfield. They are bigger, stronger, and faster; their equipment is far superior, their training methods more sensible. We think of yesterday's ballplayers as an iron man who disdained relief. Ty Cobb played fewer than 150 games in each of 16 seasons. (I am ignoring his first two part-time years of 1905 and 1906 when he played 41 games and 97 games.) The year 1965 marked the twelfth year in a row that Mays played over 150 games. Yet we disparage Mays' endurance; he has an occasional dizzy spell, he goes to the hospital for a few days, he does not start every game any more. For all the platooning, for the larger rosters of healthy, able-bodied men, today's starting ballplayer plays more than his counterpart of forty years ago.

We tend to idolize the old-timers of sport. The double-play combination of Tinker-to-Evers-to-Chance is considered the non-pareil of defensive greatness. Year in and year out Tony Kubek and Bobby Richardson made forty and fifty more double plays than the old Cub trio.

It is difficult, even impossible, to compare the players of one generation with those of another, so we are thrown back to our original standard. Judge Willie Mays not against Tris Speaker, but against perfection. Ask yourself this one question: Have you ever seen seen Willie Mays make a wrong move in the field?

Man has not yet created a perfect ballplayer. In Willie Mays, he has come mighty close.

Chapter Three

Born to Play Ball is the title of Charles Einstein's early "autobiography" of Willie Mays. It is also an extract of a remark attributed to Joe DiMaggio: "I think there are some players who are born to play ball." This is undoubtedly apocryphal; DiMaggio has never been known to say so many words in succession.

Genetics being about as reliable a science as tea-leaf reading, it is entirely possible for Willie Mays to have been born to play baseball. Willie's grandfather, Walter Mays, was a pitcher for a team in Tuscaloosa, Alabama; Willie's father, William Howard Mays, was a fine semi-pro ballplayer; and Willie's mother, Ann, had been a track star in high school. So baseball and speed have been fed into the genes of Willie Howard Mays (no, not a "Junior;" his father was "William;" Willie is "Willie," officially), and if there is any other exceptional talent, skill, or aptitude in the Mays blood, it cannot be detected by a cursory shakedown of the genealogical tree.

Willie Mays is a Negro, a southern Negro on top of that, and a product of an early broken home—all of which shows why social workers gray easily. Mays ought to have ended up in a novel about a zip-gun toting, heroin-hipped, no goodnik. He is instead a non-drink, non-smoke, reasonably well-acclimated gentleman whose major neurosis is that he is overly aggressive to a pitched baseball.

Mays was born on May 6, 1931, in a suburb of Birmingham, Alabama, called Westfield. William Howard Mays, an 18-year-old hand in a nearby steel mill, earned sometimes as much as but never more than $2,000 a year in the mill's tool room. Still, the work was steady and so was the pay, which in the early 1930's can't be knocked, even with a bat.

Willie's mother and father were divorced before Willie started grade school. The boy went on to live with his Aunt Sarah, wife of his father's brother, in a neat, middle-class five-room frame house in Fairfield, a slightly larger Birmingham suburb. Willie's mother remarried and Mays today has ten half-brothers and half-sisters by the second marriage. His mother died while giving birth to her eleventh child, Diana, in November, 1953. Willie's Aunt Sarah died in July, 1954. Willie's father is still alive.

William Howard Mays used to come home from the mill and roll a rubber ball across the floor to little Willie, aged fourteen months. Willie would push it back to his dad, and this went on for thirty or forty rolls or until the older Mays got tired of the game and quit. Whereupon, so the story goes, Willie would begin to cry.

Mays' memory of his earliest youth is confined to baseball. At the age of three, he had regular afternoon catches with his father over on the steel-mill diamond.

"But by the time he was six," his father has said, "I'd come home from work and catch him across the

street on the diamond alone, playing by himself."
Willie would toss the ball up and, with his bat, whack
it as hard as he could. Then he'd drop the bat and
run the bases, ending with a wicked slide home. He
would dust himself off, track down the ball, and give
it another ride.

According to Mays' biographer Einstein, Willie's
dream-world of that period was filled with baseball.
His idol became Joe DiMaggio, and when he played
catch with a boyhood chum, Charley Willis, Willie
would be "DiMag," or "DiMaggio."

"Throw it here," Willie would say, and Charley
Willis would lob a ball over "DiMag's" head and the
boy would race back for an over-the-shoulder grab.

For a brief spell as a boy, Willie aped DiMaggio's
classic widespread erect stance. He has since worked
out his own style, but his fairly wide stance still
faintly echoes those days when he tried to copy Joe
DiMaggio.

At about that time Willie's dad introduced him to
pepper games; standing 15 feet or so off, he rapped
ground balls of all types to the boy. It is possible
there have been outfielders with greater facility at
scooping up ground balls than Mays, but I have
never seen one. Even today, Mays in a noon-hour
pepper game is a breathtaking performer, backhand-
ing grounders with the fingertips of his immense
glove, whipping balls behind his back or through his
legs.

Willie's father was nicknamed Kitty Cat because of
his fast hands. Willie had a nickname; it was what
everybody always called him: Buckduck. Mays says

that to this day folks back home call him Buckduck. Some of the Giants call him Buck.

Mays suggests a reason for the name. "Maybe it's 'cause I used to dodge back and forth, duck so quick, when I was running." That would take care of the "duck" part. There is always the unfortunate and derogatory use of the word "buck" to denote a Negro or an American Indian male. My Oxford Universal Dictionary offers a couple other possibilities—"any animal of the antelope kind," or, "A dashing fellow; a dandy." I'll buy these; the darting antelope-swift terror on the bases, and the nattily dressed Mays who, it is alleged, insists on a crease in his baseball pants.

As a boy Willie was ordinarily big and more than ordinarily healthy. When he was ten years old, his natural talent thrust him into sandlot games with boys four and five years older. Because the best players on most pickup teams just naturally gravitate to the pitcher's mound, Mays pitched most of the time. His father casually tried to discourage it by pointing out, "Pitchers don't get to play every day, you know."

By fourteen, Willie was pitching for a semi-pro steel-mill nine. Not that the boy worked in the mill. He didn't then or ever. Once again his father was a determining force. The older Mays said he didn't care what kind of business Willie went into, but he didn't want to see the boy in the mill.

"Why not?" Willie wanted to know. "It's not such bad work. It's been all right for you."

William Howard Mays shook his head. "Once you get into the mill, you never get out."

So Willie made a few dollars pitching semi-pro ball

34

while playing basketball and football for Fairfield Industrial High. Mays took a course in cleaning and pressing at his industrial high, but never plied that trade either. He washed dishes briefly in a Birmingham cafe, where he says "folks treated me Grade-A, but I quit after one week."

Willie didn't cotton much to the academic life. Writer Joe David Brown quotes Mays, the high-schooler: "All the time my algebra teacher was saying, 'X equals how much?' I was thinking about the next ball game."

The next ball game in high school might have been the Friday night basketball game, the Saturday afternoon football game, or the Sunday semi-pro baseball contest, depending on the time of year. The boy was growing fast in high school and by the time he was 16 was pretty much all filled out, up around five-ten and 165 pounds.

In 1947, the winter he was 16, Willie led all Jefferson County players in scoring; he hit 20 or 25 points in a good night's work. High school winning teams in those days usually produced 50 or 55 points total.

Football was the same story. Willie played quarterback and fullback, did all the team's punting, kicking-off, and passing, and carried the ball on a rare sneak. Fairfield coach Jim McWilliams calls Mays "the greatest forward passer I ever saw." Willie recalls one day on the gridiron in his senior year clicking for four or five touchdown passes in a 55-0 win. He also got off 50-yard punts and even an occasional 60-yard boot, which for a 165-pound high-school boy verges on the unbelievable.

It would appear that football was the boy's greatest love. Once, when he was 13, he climbed a tree to watch Fairfield play a football game and in all the excitement fell out and broke a leg.

Another physical complaint resulted in Mays' quitting the pitcher's box for outfield play. On a hot summer's Alabama day, fourteen-year-old Willie pitched a nine-inning industrial game and broke up the contest with a last-inning home run. As he slid across home plate, he felt his head spin. His father came out of the stands and led the boy to a quiet spot where he delivered those eventful three little words: "Outfield for you."

Mays never pitched again, but he has not beaten the recurring dizzy spells. After he fainted in Cincinnati late in the 1962 season, he was thoroughly examined in a hospital and pronounced a superior physical specimen in every way. It has always been Mays' insistent opinion that he simply gets fatigued from too many ball games in which he goes all out all the time. No other judgment has come along to contradict Mays'. It is quite probably like that day he pitched nine innings and outlegged a home run; now he does not pitch but he remains constantly moving all the time in centerfield, and he continues to run bases as if his life depended on it.

Like most hometown prodigies, the time came for Willie to go outside his home and scrub team for instruction. William Howard Mays was a skilled player, as good semi-professional athletes are, and an even better instructor, but he wisely recognized there was nothing else he could give the boy.

36

Willie's future was at stake, and though it seemed likely that he could grab a football scholarship, there were two strikes against it. Willie had seen his friend Charley Willis racked up pretty badly in a high-school game, and Mays couldn't picture himself sweating through four years of "X" equaling something other than the offensive team on the blackboard.

In the spring of 1948, with Willie having just turned 17, the elder Mays took him to Lorenzo Piper Davis, manager of the Birmingham Barons of the Negro National League. Piper Davis put the youngster through his paces and signed him at $300 a season. This took Mays into direct conflict again with high-school amateur athletic participation, but the practicalities of life won out over moral judgments. As a matter of fact, Piper Davis, who insisted on the boy's finishing high school, worked out with Mays' principal a schedule whereby the boy would be released from classes for the Barons' games, but would still keep up with his work.

It would be nice to say that Mays immediately set the Negro League on fire. It would also be untrue. Nobody had to tell him much about covering the outfield; those hours of shagging flies with Charley Willis and manipulating his glove with his father had taken care of that. A story has it that Mays was impressed with the quick throwing of a Baron second baseman and began to adopt the second baseman's sidearm manner. But nobody had to teach the boy how to throw. Jack Hardy, a sweet-fielding shortstop in the league, recalls that Mays was with Birmingham just a few weeks when he made a throw nobody could quite believe. So Mays made another one a few days later, and Hardy became a believer.

At the plate it was a slightly different story. Davis fiddled with the boy's swing and style, but not to much avail. In some minor desperation Davis said early the first season, "I'll boost your pay five dollars a month for every month you're over .300." Mays collected no bonus five-spot in 1948, but if the extra pay was available in '49 and '50, he would have bankrupted Davis. He hit .316 and .350.

The early fault may have been another case of hero worship. Davis says the boy stood too close to the plate, hiding behind his left shoulder "like he was peekin' at the pitcher." It was a near-total rebellion against the earlier DiMaggio widespread classic straight-on stance. Davis kept yelling, *"Aim* on that pitcher. Don't peek at him." And Mays began to move back and open up a little, until he was halfway between the old DiMag and the new peek from around the corner. It sounds like a case of Stan Musialitis, quickly diagnosed and cured. But even with the cure Mays was not hitting with great consistency in the beginning, nor with the steady eye-popping power he would later show.

Don't get me wrong. This was a fine—an extra-fine— young prospect. The first day Mays played with the Barons, he had three hits in seven trips in a double-header. But most of the time he wasn't the Mays we know today. Not yet. But he was young and he could be taught. There has never been a manager who has had any trouble with Mays in that department. Davis was able to reach the boy with valuable tips and know-how.

Mays' talent became so ripe that if the stories can be trusted, Harry Jenkins, then director of farm personnel for the Boston Braves, started hearing reports about a boy named Willie Mays when Willie was just a thirteen-year-old sandlotter! The Braves apparently kept their eyes on him from then on and actually made an unofficial offer (it couldn't be official because Willie had not finished high school) shortly after Piper Davis took the boy under the Barons' collective wing.

The Boston offer was $7,500 for Mays' contract to be purchased from the Barons, plus another $7,500 if the boy made good within thirty days. Birmingham filed the offer and Mays kept improving, playing full years for the Barons in 1948, 1949, and part of 1950.

During one of those summers Roy Campanella, on a barnstorming club down South, saw Mays perform and immediately contacted the Dodgers' front office, recommending they take a look at the boy. Presently a Dodger scout appeared. The report said Mays looked all right in the field, but couldn't hit a curve. There is also a story that the Yankees, all-white at the time and for years to come, took a perfunctory look at Mays and agreed the boy wouldn't do.

Of Mays' days in Birmingham, one anecdote stands out. Mays has a few vices other than tormenting pitchers: western movies, action-filled television, pinball games, gin rummy, Cokes, Ella Fitzgerald records, and pool. He has become a fairly proficient pool player, his progress hastened by his years with Leo Durocher.

When Mays and Marghuerite Wendelle Kenny Chapman set up housekeeping in an opulent, mirrored, chandeliered and brocaded upper Manhattan house, a velvet-smooth pool table slid naturally into Mays' game room.

A game of pool back in the Barons' days cast new light on the Mays personality. One night he got so involved trying to wrap the corner pocket around the four ball that the team bus got tired of waiting for the centerfielder and took off for a game in St. Louis. Miles down the pavement the bus driver saw a taxi start to fill his rear-view mirror until the cabby was alongside, flagging him down. Willie Mays was leaning from the rear window, screaming:

"What you gonna do? You gonna leave me? I'm a pro ballplayer, hear! You can't leave me."

Not much of a story, but indicative not only of Mays's passion for the sport (and for pool), but of another quality not often hinted at—his chagrin that people had not waited for him, had not seen to it that he was on the bus, even though it was obviously his fault that he wasn't. Despite all Mays' geniality, his complete lack of affectation, he still has a touch of pride that probably grew out of the rock-hard sandlot diamonds of Alabama when he was just a tyke with a too-large fielder's mitt and too many people oohed and aahed at his cavorting.

Mays got to St. Louis with the Barons that day and, with Sunday off, took in a St. Louis Browns-Boston

Red Sox game, where he stared open-jawed at Ted Williams at bat. This may have helped as much as anything in getting Mays out of his Musial bends.

Even before Willie had established himself as much more than a pretty fair hand with the Barons, there were knocks on the door. First, of course, was the Boston Brave offer of $7,500 and another "perhaps" $7,500. Then the Chicago White Sox made a modest bid. Lastly, the New York Giants wandered onto the scene inadvertently and suddenly submitted the most attractive and final bid.

This is a story told often, retold here to keep the chronology honest. On the recommendation of Alex Pompez, who used to scout the Negro leagues and now searches out the Caribbean area for baseball talent for the Giants, a couple of Giants scouts, Ed Montague and Bill Harris, hied themselves to Birmingham to see whether the Barons' first baseman Alonzo (Lou) Perry might fill a spot on the Giants' Sioux City farm team, then in the Class A Western League.

After the game Montague and Harris decided that Sioux City would have to get along without Perry, but they sure liked the centerfielder. Montague put through a phone call to Jack Schwarz, lieutenant to Carl Hubbell, Giant farm director. Sputtered Montague, "I saw a young kid of an outfielder I can't believe. He can hit, run, and throw like—like nobody. Don't ask any questions. Just grab the boy."

Schwarz asked some questions, then put in a direct call to the Baron owner, offering a flat $10,000 for Mays' contract. Birmingham liked that better than

41

the bird-in-the-bush deal of the Braves, and the day after Willie was graduated from Fairfield Industrial High in 1950, Montague came to the door with all the necessary papers. Included was an additional $2,-000 for Willie—inducement to sign in haste. The youngster and William Howard Mays huddled briefly, and then the older Mays said it wasn't enough; they wanted $6,000. Montague telephoned Horace Stoneham, and Stoneham said to give the boy the money.

With the receipt of this informal bonus, the last element of a tall tale is laid to rest—the tale that Willie Mays is disdainful of receiving wages for his services. The legend has been somewhat wistfully stitched together by Giant publicity men, famous for promoting this sort of selflessness in their employees. One stubborn myth had Carl Hubbell receiving a signed contract each winter with the space for his next year's salary left blank. Hub would then fill in what he thought he deserved, always a modest sum indeed. The Giant organization is paternalistic and at times charmingly ineffectual, but it has never been known to throw money away needlessly. Shortly after the Giants moved to San Francisco, its stock was listed on the exchange at $900 a share, a jump of 600% in three years, and it has gone up since. Inasmuch as Horace Stoneham himself owns some 9,000 shares, disdain over monetary matters among Giant executives is as unlikely as a catcher's mask on an Eskimo bride. Ballplayers too are naturally aware of the financial facts of life.

Mays certainly plays ball for money. From the moment he discovered that his father was getting paid for those fast hands, he has always expected a *quid pro quo* relationship with his bosses. Today he is the highest-paid baseball player around. He receives more money in salary than any player in the history of the game. More than Ruth, Musial, Williams, DiMaggio, or Mantle. When the 1965 season was in the books, it was rumored that Mays was going to ask for $150,000 the following year! Nonsense. All he asked for—and got—was $130,000!

Chapter Four

The most important event in baseball history this century has not been the introduction of the lively ball, or the shift of franchises, or the innovation of divisional playoffs in each league. It has not been the White Sox scandal or the emergence of Babe Ruth or the decline, fall, and rise of the spitball. It is not Casey Stengel. It was the signing of Jackie Robinson to a baseball contract in October, 1945, by the Brooklyn Dodger organization, and the subsequent use of other Negro ball players in the majors.

Baseball today is one of the more integrated communities in America, and it is becoming more so as pressures on southern winter-training bases force an end to separate, unequal living arrangements for visiting white and Negro players. With the Braves in Atlanta, the South is falling fast to the demands and moralities of contemporary history. Even if the South does not totally yield to this pressure, it won't matter much. Teams will simply do more and more of their training in Arizona and Palm Springs.

My interest here is not so much in this ethnic development as in the influence of Negroes on the playing field. If you want to see how foolish baseball experts can sound when they pontificate on matters beyond their ken, here is an editorial from the *Sport-*

ing News, baseball's trade journal, of an old August, 1942, number:

"There is no law against Negroes playing with white teams, nor whites with colored teams, but neither has invited the other for the obvious reason that they prefer to draw their talent from their own ranks and because the leaders of both groups know their crowd psychology and do not care to run the risk of damaging their own game. Other sports had a Joe Louis, Jesse Owens, Fritz Pollard, and other notables, respected and honored by all races, but they competed under different circumstances from those dominating baseball.

"The baseball fan is a peculiar creature. He deems it his inalienable right and privilege to criticize and jeer in words that not always are the choicest or the most gentlemanly. Not even a Ted Williams or a Joe DiMaggio or a Babe Ruth is immune. It is not difficult to imagine what would happen if a player on a mixed team, performing before a crowd of the opposite color, should throw a beanball, strike out with the bases full or spike a rival. Clear-minded men of tolerance of both races realize the tragic possibilities and have steered clear of such complications, because they realize it is to the benefit of each and also of the game."

I am gradually evolving a theory that the calibre of a baseball team is in direct proportion to the number of Negroes on its roster. I owe a debt to writers Joe Reichler and Allison Danzig for backing up my theory with facts which I have lifted from their mammoth volume, *The History of Baseball.*

Reichler and Danzig point out that since Jackie Robinson entered the majors in 1947, Negroes won nine of the next fourteen Most Valuable Player awards presented by the Baseball Writers Association to National League players: Robinson himself, Roy Campanella (three times), Mays, Don Newcombe, Hank Aaron, and Ernie Banks (twice).

Negroes keep winning the NL Most Valuable Player award: Bob Gibson in 1968, Orlando Cepeda the year before, Mays (for the second time) in 1965, Maury Wills in 1962, and Frank Robinson in 1961. Once I asked the pitcher Gene Conley, who had worked in both leagues, what was the one major difference between the two leagues.

"Color," he said. "Know what I mean?" Certainly I knew. The difference between the two leagues—then —was the larger number of talented Negroes in the National League. Things have since leveled off; the two leagues are very close in quality. Why? The American League has begun to catch up with the National League in talented black ballplayers. In the American League, of the top five hitters for average in 1969, four were black. In the National League, in 1969, four of the top five were black.

Jackie Robinson broke the ground for Willie Mays. And because of the peculiar nature of the Giant-Dodger feud, it became almost mandatory that the Giants secure talented Negroes, once Robinson had proved himself with the Dodgers. Whatever the Dodgers did, the Giants had to do at least as well. In this case, business sense dictated it. If the Dodgers cornered the early market in talented Negro players, what would happen to the huge Negro population all about the Polo Grounds? Would they stop attending Giant games?

In 1951, when Willie Mays entered the major leagues, the ideal place for a Negro to play baseball was not only in the National League, not only in New York, but particularly in Manhattan and most particularly at the Polo Grounds.

I was born in a hospital on St. Nicholas Avenue and lived my first four years in an apartment house at 155th Street and Edgecombe Avenue, approximately one long downwind spit from the Polo Grounds. This was back in the early 1920's, and the neighborhood— today you'd call it the north edge of Harlem—was pure and sallow. I recall, without much understanding, the whispers and then the cries, "The Negroes are coming! The Negroes are coming!" (except these paragons did not say "Negroes"). Pretty soon—1926, 1927—the whites had fled for the sanctity of the Bronx, where all they had to worry about were the beer wars of Dutch Schultz and Mad Dog Coll, who gunned down babies in the street.

But before I fled, I used to go to Giant games. Even then there was a sprinkling of Negroes in the audience. When I rode in later years on the Independent subway to the Polo Grounds, the train cars used to be half and half, maybe darker than that. And when I sat in the Polo Grounds bleachers on September 29, 1957, the last day the Giants played in New York, three-fourths of the bleacherites (a word ironically derived from "to whiten") were Negro.

The Negroes had come. And New York Giant baseball was the richer for it. So is San Francisco baseball today. So, indeed, is baseball. Imagine the Chicago Cubs without Ernie Banks, the Braves without Aaron, the Dodgers without Wills, and the Giants without Mays.

I do not pretend there is anything about Negro genes that make for a better ballplayer. That would be not only inverse bigotry, but utter nonsense. My theory that Negroes have lifted the calibre of baseball is based on a simple numbers game. There will be more good ballplayers in a lot of a thousand Negro and white youths than in a lot of five hundred white youths alone.

By the time Willie Mays reached the Giants in 1951, the time, place, team and fandom were ready for him.

Mays may have been less ready, however. America's concern in matters of racial change has always been with the white man who finds a Negro next to him on the job, in union halls, at lunch counters, in schools, on the ball field, at the polling place. We try to accommodate the white man so that he will accept this new part of his life, yet in many cases, it is the Negro who must make the greater psychological adjustment.

Willie Mays came from a Negro community, went to a Negro school. When he played high school football and basketball it was on non-integrated teams against other non-integrated teams. His father's steel-mill club, the United Steelworkers (CIO), was an all-Negro team, and the joke was that "CIO" stood for "colored industrial only."

When Mays was signed to his first professional ball contract, it was with the Birmingham Barons, usually referred to as the Birmingham Black Barons. When he stepped out of the Barons for winter barnstorming down South, he travelled on jim crow trains, went to jim crow rest rooms, ate at jim crow restaurants, drank from jim crow fountains. Mays met and played with such ball players as Monte Irvin, Henry Thompson, Curt Roberts, and Roy Campanella, all Negroes. When he was 17, he batted against Satchel Paige (and went one for two, but then Satch was already going downhill fast that year—1948, the same year the Cleveland Indians decided he was good enough for the majors).

After Mays' graduation from Fairfield Industrial High in Alabama, he was shipped to Trenton, New Jersey, in the Interstate (Class B) League, property of the New York Giant organization. At Trenton he was thrust into what was for him a new kind of baseball—integrated, yes, but nearly all the players were white. It was not a completely foreign experience. On tours Mays had played in parks such as the Polo Grounds, so he did know some rights denied him down South. But New York was not a mecca of racial tolerance.

When Jackie Robinson joined Montreal, playing under a Mississippi-born white man, he immediately began to spray hits in all directions. It may have been a case of the dedicated passionate Robinson trying to prove not only himself, but his whole race. When Mays reached Trenton, the day of trial for the race was over. If Mays made good or not, it no longer mattered, except to Mays. And Mays was not only a rookie ballplayer; he was a Negro pushed into a startlingly different environment. The first twenty-two times Mays batted for Trenton, he made outs.

Mays dragged himself to his manager, Bill McKechnie, Jr., son of the former old-time Indianapolis slugger and successful National League manager.

Mays said, "How'm I going to hit this pitching?"

"Don't worry about it," young McKechnie said; "you don't strike me as the worrying kind."

"I'm not," Mays said.

"Well, don't start in now. Just go up there and take your swings." Mays took his swings and in his remaining trips to the plate hit around .380. I don't know how to explain the slump, except by pointing out that he may have been worried *before* he took his first swing—a perfectly normal reaction for a nineteen-year-old Negro in a brave new pale-faced world.

Mays ended his first year in the Giant organization with a .353 batting average in 81 games. In one respect it is a slightly deceiving figure. He hit only four home runs in his 306 times at bat. This is a home run every 75 trips or so, as compared with his major-league pace of a home run each 15 trips. Mays was hitting for average, but apparently not for distance. Yet he had 55 runs batted in, 20 doubles, and eight triples—figures which work out over a full season to a 100 RBI's, 35 or more doubles, and 14 or 15 triples. The speed was there, indicated not so much by his seven stolen bases, as by those triples. You cannot hit three-baggers with any consistency unless you can fly.

Still, this was all class B. In the spring of 1951,

Willie Mays reported to Sanford, Florida, to work out with his new team, Minneapolis, in the American Association, on a Triple-A club. The jump was a long one. Mays not only made it; he landed on the other side.

In spring training that year, Mays' new manager, former outfielder Tommy Heath, one evening brought into the Miller dressing room the then-most-important member of the parent Giants, Leo Durocher, manager of the New York club picked by many experts to win the National League pennant. In 1950 the Giants had finished third, coming on with a rush, thanks to strong pitching and some dandy work around second base by Eddie Stanky and Alvin Dark. It was the kind of ball club that Durocher likes to call "my type of team"—fast, smart, stingy, but not overly muscular.

Durocher shook hands with Mays and said, "Heard a lot about you. Maybe I'll be seeing you around." Then he went down the line, squeezed more palms and escaped.

Durocher had indeed heard about Mays. Durocher is no fool. He is one of the brainiest men in baseball. Mays' prior feats at Trenton had reached Durocher's attention; young, swift, powerful minor-leaguers represent the future of a ball club. In 1950 a Giant scout named Chick Genovese had one day collared Leo Durocher in Wilkes Barre, Pennsylvania, and filled Durocher's ear with the doings of a young kid named Mays on the Trenton farm. Still, even if he had been widely apprised of the youngster's potential, nobody would have predicted how immediately the Giants would be seeing the boy around.

The 1951 baseball campaign reeks with memorabilia. With another bow to historians Danzig and Reichler, I cite it as the year a midget lugged a bat to the plate at Sportsmen's Park in St. Louis, the year Allie Reynolds pitched two no-hitters and Bob Feller grabbed off his third, the year Joe DiMaggio quit baseball ... and Willie Mays joined the Giants.

Willie Mays made his first appearance in a New York Giant uniform 36 games after the pennant play had got underway. During those 36 games a small but growing baseball world gradually began to notice that outside the majors a fuss was developing over an otherwise unknown ballplayer. By the time Mays came up, the fuss was a large ado. Bruce Dudley, president of the American Association, called the youngster "the most sensational rookie ever to break into the big league." Mays was, as the cliche makers say, a "pheenom." With two "e"s, please.

I own a sixty-two page booklet titled *Baseball Lingo,* put out by the makers of Phillies cigars, which contains definitions of common baseball expressions and cliches. "Pheenom," the booklet says, is "modern lingo for a highly-touted rookie, coined by Garry Schumacher of the Giants and first applied to Clint Hartung just after World War II. Hartung did not live up to expectations (to put it kindly!), the result being that 'pheenom' has since had a skeptical connotation. 'Pheenom' is a slang contraction of the adjective 'phenomenal,' which was frequently applied to heralded rookies."

The influence of Garry Schumacher has been widely felt through sporting America, but *Baseball Lingo* has made a slight error. On June 29, 1907, the Washington *Post* began a story:

"Manager Joe Cantillon has added a young phenom to his staff. The young man's name is Walter Johnson...." True, that "phenom" had only one "e" and *Baseball Lingo's* has two, but this is nit-picking indeed.

The slang abortive "phenom" has had a rich past, pre-dating Garry Schumacher's usage by nearly 40 years. The ease with which the *Post* slides in the word leads me to believe that "phenom" had been in the sportswriter's arsenal of homily many years before the 1907 dispatch. Rich past or not, Walter Johnson or no, *Baseball Lingo's* point is well taken: heralded rookies have a habit of coming unglued from their royal frockings.

And as for Willie Mays? In thirty-five games with the Minneapolis Millers of the American Association, Mays was a two "e," even a three "e" pheenom. He hit .477 with the Millers, 71 hits in 149 appearances; 71 hits in 35 games. Over two hits per game! Of his 71 hits, there were 18 doubles, three triples, and eight home runs. Had Mays kept up that pace for an entire season, he would have ended with some 70 doubles, 10 or 15 triples, and 30 home runs, plus another 165 or 170 singles. Around 460-470 total bases.

None of this is to suggest that the month Mays spent at Minneapolis proves his skill as a major league player. No matter how good the brand of ball in a Triple A league, it is not the majors. But you can see why Mays' reputation preceded him when he joined the Giants.

Still, for every Walter Johnson, there are five dozen Clint Hartungs. In every spring-training camp every year, some rookie muscles his way into the sports headlines, only to fade from sight within weeks. Perhaps Mays himself recognized the trap in minor-league greatness. In his autobiography he and Charles Einstein relate Mays' uncertainty, even unhappiness with the call to drop his Minneapolis uniform and catch the first plane East.

The Millers had just finished a home stay and were preparing for an exhibition game in Sioux City. The night before, Mays took in a movie, and while he was enjoying the Western, the manager of the theatre stepped onto the stage, paged Mays, and told him to look up his manager, Tommy Heath, at the hotel. As Einstein tells it, Mays found Heath in his room, holding out his hand and grinning.

"Congratulations!" he said.

"What for?" Mays said.

"You're going up to the big league."

"Who said so?"

"Durocher," Heath said. "That's who."

"Not me," Mays said. "Call up Durocher and tell him I'm not coming."

When Heath realized Mays was serious, he phoned Durocher in New York and explained the boy's reluctance. Durocher told Heath to put Mays on.

"What do you mean, you're not coming up?" Durocher said.

"I mean it. I can't play that kind of ball."

"What can't you do?"

"I can't hit that kind of pitching."

"What are you hitting for Minneapolis now?" (As if Durocher didn't know).

"Four seventy-seven."

Durocher said quietly, "Do you think you could hit half that for me?" So Mays went East.

In March, 1961, I queried Mays about this conversation and he swears it happened just so.

"I was scared," Mays recalled. "I really didn't want to go." He added something that leads me to believe a coat of rationalization has partly obscured the memory of the phone call:

"I didn't want to go because I knew there'd be more pressure on me, joining a team that was going bad. The Giants were in a losing streak, and they'd be looking to me."

This is not quite accurate. The Giants *had* been going bad. That year they'd won their first game, then lost one, then won a game and lost 11 in a row. This left them with two wins and 12 losses—so deep in the cellar that Durocher's type of team was developing diver's bends. But since then, the Giants had recovered nicely, winning 15 of their next 22 games. You win pennants at that pace.

This is the way the National League pennant race looked on the morning of May 25, 1951, the day Mays joined the Giants in Philadelphia:

	WON	LOST	GAMES BEHIND
BROOKLYN	20	13	—
ST. LOUIS	18	15	2
CHICAGO	17	15	2½
BOSTON	18	17	3
NEW YORK	17	19	4½
PHILADELPHIA	16	18	4½
CINCINNATI	15	19	5½
PITTSBURGH	14	19	6

This is no great record, but for a club that had lost 12 of its first 14 games, it isn't bad, and four-and-a-half games out of first place in late May isn't much of a handicap.

I suspect Mays' reluctance to make the big move had to do with the same sort of internal pressure that had beset him when the Giants snatched him from the Barons and shoved him into the lineup at Trenton. This new move would be, in baseball terms, the biggest change, the longest jump he'd ever have to make. Mays was, as he says, scared, but not because the Giants were going bad. The fear was personal.

Not that the Giants didn't need Mays. They needed him—or someone—badly, despite the late rush they had recently engineered. The Giant centerfielder was Bobby Thomson, hitting .229 the night Mays stepped into the lineup. I suspect Mays had heard about his joining the Giants well before his night at the movies. It has been reported that even before the Giants had reached an 11-game losing streak, Durocher sensed his team wasn't quite as solid as he had first believed and had asked that Mays be brought to the Giants immediately. Horace Stoneham did not think Mays was ready for the majors. "Anyway," Stoneham is said to have added, "he's due to go into the Army at any minute."

The Giant losing streak grew and Durocher kept after Stoneham until Stoneham relented. It is likely, if all this is true, that word kept filtering out to Minneapolis that the Giants were thinking of bringing up Mays, and Willie probably had a couple of weeks to worry over the forthcoming move.

Even if Mays didn't want to go (and in a way he very definitely didn't), this was nothing compared to the discontent of Miller fans at the thought of Willie's leaving. The feeling was so strong that Horace Stoneham had to take out, in the local Minneapolis press, quarter-page ads that reeked with sincerity and read in part:

"We appreciate Mays' worth to the Millers, but in all fairness, Mays himself must be a factor in these considerations. Merit must be recognized. On the records of his performance since the American Association season started, Mays is entitled to his promotion, and the chance to prove that he can play major league baseball. It would be most unfair to deprive him of the opportunity he earned with his play.

"We honestly admit, too, that this player's exceptional talents are the exact answer to the Giants' most critical need."

The exact answer arrived the night of May 25, 1951, nineteen days past Willie's 20th birthday. He stood then a quarter-inch short of five feet eleven inches. He weighed 180 pounds, or about five more than when he joined Trenton eleven months before. He had behind him a total of 116 games in organized baseball, or not even a full year of minor-league experience.

He wore his gray flannel Giant travelling uniform lower that night than he does today, because Leo Durocher had not got around to tipping him off—he would in a few days—that long, low trouser legs give the pitcher and the umpire a larger strike zone.

He wore his cap then, as he does today, tilted forward so that instead of the rear band slipping over the crown of his skull and grasping the lower rear part of the head just below it, the band rode high on the crown, teetering, and the wonder is not that the cap falls off so much but that it stays on at all. There is reason for nearly everything Mays does on the ball field. He tips his cap forward because it shades his eyes more effectively from the sun glare and the arc lights.

He used an extra-big fielder's glove then, as he does today, because he has extra-large hands. Today Giant ballplayers like to give their new gloves to Mays to break in; his hand is that much larger than their own. (One suspects a little superstition too: the hope that some defensive magic will stick to the glove. Mays himself is not free from such superstitions. Monte Irvin, who was Mays' roommate with the Giants, remembers that once when Mays dropped a fly ball, he slapped his glove and said sharply, "Shame on you for not catching that ball.")

Mays did not wear the glove then the way he does

today. Today he slips his fingers only partly into the glove, the way a first baseman does, and for precisely the same reason. This way he gains inches of reach, and the fingertip catch of a line drive into right-centerfield can be attributed mainly to Mays' speed, timing and leap, but also to the extra inches of glove reaching for the ball.

When Willie Mays stepped to the batting cage for his first practice licks, the players in Shibe Park—both Giants and Phillies, Lockman and Irvin, Dark and Thomson, Willie Jones, Richie Ashburn, and Eddie Waitkus, all of them—stopped doing what they had been doing, and a hush fell over the playing field. As Russ Hodges, Giant radio and TV play-by-play announcer, reverently recalls it, "Willie began to comb the ball," hitting line drives straight as spikes, as the awe deepened, until Leo Durocher said, "I swear, I'm going to marry that boy!"

Chapter Five

The *New York Times* of May 26, 1951—the morning after Willie Mays had made his baseball introduction as a Giant—began a John Drebinger bylined story this way:

"Inspired by the presence of their flashy rookie star, Willie Mays, the Giants rallied for five runs in the eighth inning . . ."

The Giants had won a ball game, with Willie Mays in their lineup and batting third. And what had Mays done, after combing three balls in batting practice into the leftfield seats? The first time he stood quietly by as right-handed Bubba Church curved a ball over the outside corner, and Mays was called out on strikes. The next four times he went out. Oh-for-five. In the ninth inning Mays had run into Monte Irvin, and a fly ball by Eddie Waitkus fell for a two-base hit.

It is hard to imagine a more inauspicious debut. Yet there was Drebinger, in the coolest, least emotional of all newspapers, leading off his piece with Willie Mays, who had done nothing.

Earlier I advanced the theory that New York was exactly the right place and 1951 the right time for Willie Mays. Not only because of the color of his skin. Ball clubs have historical personalities. In New

York there were three ball clubs. The Yankees throughout their history, and especially at that moment were cold, colorless perfectionists, the swift, skilled executioners who never made a mistake. The Dodgers had been bumbling, fumbling clowns, stigmatized by the sight of two baserunners on one base or outfielders struck on the head and shoulders by fly balls, and even their success in the 1940's had not removed the secret shame of the Dodgers and Dodger fans. Withal, they were a boisterous bragging ball club, a club that seldom beat you with its talents, but might with its heart, is bully-boy tactics, its fierce *braggadocio.*

The Giants had been a proud rollicking crew, for years as good as—better than—the best, always with a flair, a spirit, so that they combined the best features of both the Yankee and Dodger ball clubs, talent and combativeness. But that was the dimming past. When the 1950 season ended, the Giants had completed the longest dry spell in the post-1900 history of the organization. For thirteen years no pennant had flown at the Polo Grounds. Never had a Giant team gone so long without water. The longest previous drought had been the eight years from 1925 through 1932, and during that period the Giants had three times finished second and three times third. During this thirteen-year spell, beginning with the year after Bill Terry's Giants won consecutive pennants in 1936 and 1937, no Giant team had come as close as second. Nine times the Giants had finished in the second division. Twice they'd been last.

In the National League only one other team had

not won a pennant during the same thirteen years—
the Pittsburgh Pirates, then entering into a full-
stinkweed period as perhaps the worst team the league
had ever seen. Yet during the thirteen-year period the
Pirates twice finished second!

With some ball clubs this winless stretch might not
have seemed so crushing as it was to both Giant
owners and Giant fans. The Giants were not used to
losing. In the first half-century through 1950—in fact,
during the first 37 years of the century—Giant teams
had won thirteen National League pennants. In those
37 years before the Giants started losing with the
dreary regularity of an insomniac's ticking clock, no
team had won more often. The Yankees had won just
nine pennants in those 37 years and had once gone 18
years without winning. The vaunted Philadelphia
Athletics had won pennants four times in five years,
ending in 1914, and had then finished dead last seven
times in succession!

Over that period the New York Giants were baseball's finest team—swifter, more powerful, smarter,
fiercer than any other, a ball club that had somehow
combined the quiet princely skill of Mathewson and
the fury of McGraw. Now the club's personality lay
like clay, dormant, dull, dispirited.

There had been some brief hope for this 1951 club.
After all, it had done reasonably well in 1950, finishing third and climbing the backs of the winners at
the close. In Durocher it had a manager who closely
resembled McGraw (I'm sorry if this offends you,
Old-timer) , and personnel in whom the manager had
confidence.

Then came the eleven-game losing streak at the outset, last place, and bitterly cynical fans pouring their abusive thunder on the heads of Durocher and his type of ballplayer. Sometimes a slim shard of hope came to life in the form of a new rookie (Johnny Rucker, Clint Hartung), a purchased star (the $175,-000 Walker Cooper), or dogged spirit (Eddie Stanky). Each time the hope had to be buried. And as the drought lengthened, the years turning into a decade and the decade threatening to turn into a score, the Giants—owners, fans, team, even hardened baseball writers—reached frantically for any straw.

In 1951 the Giants were waiting for Willie Mays. On no other club—not even the Dodgers, that perfectly tailored bandbox where he might have hit 50 home runs every year—was he so needed, hoped for.

The Giants got Mays on May 25, and he went oh-for-five. On the wings of just his name, his slight previous fame, his bubbling youth, his spirit, even on the fact that in his oh-for-five he had twice made out on long fly balls (so Drebinger enthusiastically told his readers), the club took heart and took flight.

They won May 25th, 8-5. They won the next day, 2-0, and Mays went oh-for-three (but he walked twice, Drebinger cheerfully noted). They won the next day too for a clean sweep of the Philadelphia series, and Mays went oh-for-four. He had not made a hit in his first twelve times at bat. But what difference did it make—the Giants were over .500 for the first time! And now they moved into New York, where Mays would be really home, and watch him go!

On May 28, 1951, still batting third, Mays stepped

in for his first licks at the Polo Grounds, and Warren Spahn threw a fast ball, slightly inside, the high hard one. Mays swung, the ball rose on a mighty line and headed over the left-field roof, a few feet fair.

The Giants lost, 4-1, and Mays didn't make another hit after the home run off Spahn in his next thirteen times at bat. Mays' one hit in twenty-six appearances had him at .039 and should have ended any hope. On May 30, having gone hitless in two at-bats, his calf muscles tightened and Mays had to quit a game. When he went out, the dedicated few were glad to see him go.

And yet ... There was something about the boy (twenty years old, not nineteen, as the writers kept saying and still insist whenever they recreate that spring), something that made him just a little different from those other failures—Rucker, Hartung. They didn't know it then, but we—with the greatest of all senses, hindsight—do. He had quicksilver.

To say that Mays was disheartened by his start would be telling the truth, but to say that it crushed him would be laying it on a little thick. He told his manager that he didn't think he would ever hit, that he was doing the team no good and ought to be taken out of the lineup. But Durocher, gambler, plunger, card shark, pool hero and shrewd appraiser of the spirit, told the boy to relax, he would start hitting, he was still his centerfielder, the best centerfielder he'd ever seen, that if Willie didn't make another hit all season, he'd still be his boy.

Mays promptly went on a binge, directly from his one-for-26 spell; he hit .375 for a while, shoved his batting average above .315, slipped back again to a respectable .275 and there, a few points more or less, he stayed.

In the field, Mays was Mays. He charged ground-ball base hits as no outfielder ever before had charged them. Sometimes he overcharged them; the ball was through in that yawning Polo Grounds centerfield, and singles became triples or even inside-the-park home runs. Sometimes he fumbled them, so eager, so headlong the rush, and runners advanced a base.

But most often, many, many times more often than not, the hours and years of pepper games, Kitty Cat and Buckduck showed, and soon base runners acted as if they were nailed to basepaths. The word raced through the league on legs swifter than Sam Jethroe's; you can't run on this boy Mays. And in that first month or two, a rookie had revolutionized outfielding play. Outfielders today must be short-stops in their approach to ground-ball base hits.

That was coming in on balls. Going out was the same story. Mays played the shallowest centerfield since Tris Speaker (and Speaker spent most of those years behind shortstop in the days of the dead ball), and yet how many times have balls hit over Mays' head and not caught by him remained in play? The Vic Wertz catch in the 1954 World Series—more on that later—is the classic example of Mays' ability to go straight back and outrun the most distant, savage-ly-hit drives.

Sure, Mays ran down Monte Irvin on occasion, or Don Mueller. Sure, he hogged fly balls, roamed all three fields. He has since learned to patrol his territory and let the others handle their own beats. But again the effect was electrifying. It reminded one of the old Pirate outfield in the days of Paul and Lloyd Waner, of how the Waner brothers, especially Lloyd, seemed to cover all three fields. Yet they were two, and Mays was one, and that too is the difference between Mays and the rest of the outfielders any of us has ever seen. It was just as Mays' former manager, Tommy Heath, said in that tired cliché: "He covers centerfield like a tent."

And throw, how he could—can—throw! Mostly, he could get rid of the ball. In his glove, snatched away and gone, like that. They talk about infielders who have quick hands, who gobble up ground balls and have them on their way to first so swiftly you barely see the full motion. There is a standing joke among Pittsburgh Pirate ballplayers that Bill Mazeroski will never wear out a glove, because ground balls are never in the pocket long enough to make a dent, so fast are Maz's hands in sending the ball on its way either to first for the out or to second for the force. Mays is like that, and among outfielders supreme, aided as he is now with his basket catch, the ball grabbed in front of him near his waist, then drawn back and thrown. Other outfielders catch fly balls up around the shoulders and then must dip their arm to the waist before drawing back and letting go.

And so it came to pass, Mays and the Giants, in 1951. The Giants as a whole played fair ball, a little better than .500, from the end of May until that moment in August when the pennant race really began. The Dodgers had gone hot, and on August 11 when Brooklyn won the first game of a double-header while the Giants were losing to Philadelphia, the second-place Giants trailed Brooklyn by 13½ games. Then the Dodgers lost their nightcap and the lead was 13.

This is how the two teams looked when August 11, 1951, was in the books:

	WON	LOST	GAMES BEHIND
BROOKLYN	70	36	
NEW YORK	59	51	13

And so, for the 1951 season, hope was dead again. The Giants couldn't win. Brooklyn radiocaster Red Barber, most literate, most intelligent of that day's play-by-play announcers, made the iconoclastic and nervy gesture of wondering over the air one afternoon just what was the earliest date a National League club had clinched a pennant. Weren't the Dodgers, Red wanted to know, likely to beat the date?

No. Beginning on August 12 the Giants went on a 16-game winning streak, nearly every game a heart-clutcher. From the scores of those 16 victories, you can see how tight most of the contests were: 3-2, 2-1, 5-2, 4-2, 3-1, 2-1, 8-5, 2-0, 5-4, 7-4, 4-3, 6-5, 5-4, 5-1, 5-4 and 6-3. The biggest margin was four runs. The Giants had won eight games by one run.

Tight baseball means a team has one quality absolutely imperative in winning—glue. The team that plays together stays together, or something. With Bob Thomson at third and Lockman at first, Monte Irvin in left, and Don Mueller in right, and with the strongest down-the-middle defense in baseball—Westrum, Dark and Stanky, and Willie Mays, this Giant team had glue. No Giant starting lineup since, not even the 1954 marvels, has had as much glue. In 1954 the Giant bench was the difference. In 1951 it was a team effort of a varsity nine. For the first time since 1937, the Giants were adhered into a smoothly meshing unit.

It is not necessarily true that Willie Mays made the difference. But he was the only vitally different member of the 1951 lineup over the 1950 team.

This brings us to the play of that 1951 season. Some call it the best Willie Mays ever made, which could make it the best of our time. *Time* Magazine called it "The Throw." On August 15, the winning streak barely discernible—the Giants had won four in a row, the Giants and Dodgers were tied at the Polo Grounds, 1-1, eighth inning, one out, Billy Cox on third base, Ralph Branca on first and Carl Furillo up. In the stands there were 21,007 fans wondering whether, with the Giant win yesterday, the Giants were finally learning how to beat the Dodgers, and wasn't it a pity they were—*if* they were—learning too late. In 16 games that year between the two rivals, Brooklyn had won 12 times.

Furillo hit a fly ball into right centerfield. Mays, playing over in left-center for the notorious pull-hitting Furillo, had to come a long distance to make the catch. Make it he did, on the dead run, gloved hand extended, and that was two out, but Billy Cox on third had tagged up and was heading home with the lead run. And Cox could run.

Whitey Lockman had slipped into the cut-off spot on a line between the ball and home plate ("He ought to hire out as a bombsight," a newsman said later), so that if Mays caught the fly and made his throw homeward, Lockman would be in a position to cut down Branca just in case the Dodger pitcher broke for second on Mays' throw to the plate. It was a routine move for Lockman, for any first-baseman, but it made the play.

When Mays caught the fly ball, running full speed toward the right-field foul line, he was moving away from the play. If he stopped dead and threw, he could not possibly get any zip on the ball. So he improvised. He caught the ball, planted his left foot, and pivoted *away* from the play—that is, to his left, counter-clockwise—so that for a flashing moment his back was to home plate, his face to the centerfield bleacherites, who must have wondered what in heck the boy was doing, dancing like that. Then, coming full around in his pivot, he let the ball fly, taking dead aim at the letters on Whitey Lockman's flannel shirt. The ball cut air like a bullet; Mays' spin had, much like a discus-tosser's, added momentum to the throw.

Lockman allowed the ball to go through to Westrum, and Billy Cox, sliding desperately, was out. For a long second the stands were silent, not quite certain they had seen right. Then they exploded.

Eddie Brannick has called the play "the greatest I've ever seen," and Brannick, oldest of the Giant officials, has seen just about every great play made in a Giant ball park the past fifty years or so.

Mays himself called it his finest throw; Charlie Dressen, then Dodger manager, says Mays would have to do it again before he'd believe it; and Furillo said flatly that the play was impossible, and that was that.

In the last half of the inning, Mays—up first, to succor the hearts of the superstitious who insist a man who's made a great play in the field always bats first in his team's half—singled, Wes Westrum hit a home run, and the Giants had their 3-1 win. One might say that because the regular season ended in a tie, this single ball game, this Throw, made the difference, but, of course, had Cox been safe and everything else followed as it did, the Giants would still have won, 3-2. It didn't matter in the long run, in the story of Mays' greatness, his value to club. Win or lose, it was not apparent that Mays had lifted the ball club.

And with the Giants running hard at the Dodgers, fame—another manifestation of it—came to 20-year-old Willie Mays. Soon he was pursued by all the latchers-on-to-glory: the athlete-hungry girls, the sycophantic back-slappers, the parasitic newspapermen hanging around for an exclusive on Willie's love life, his private thoughts, his closeted fears and dreams. And of course the ad men came full tilt, pens held high and dollar bills streaming. All Willie had to do was sign. Breakfast foods, cigarettes, razor blades, bubble gum sought his endorsement, in the hope that if Willie Mays said he liked *Carcigens,* the least cancer-making smoke, or *Stickums,* the loudest popping bubble gum of all, then all America would go to their graves with a Carcigen plastered to their lips and, in their back pocket, a Stickum wrapper, its fortune reading: "You smoke too much."

The Giants did what they could to protect their *wunderkind*. Frank Forbes, New York boxing official and former great Negro athlete, was asked to cluck Willie over the rough patches in the road. Forbes found the boy an apartment in Harlem where the meals were good and regular. He steered him to an agency to handle all the ad men. Interviews had to be cleared with the agency. And Forbes himself watched the boy. Once, it has been said, Forbes had to knock an ice-cream soda into a woman's lap to upset a particularly intimate relationship on which he frowned. That would be Mays: romance at the soda fountain.

Forbes has explained, in round rich euphony, his role in the Willie Mays-Giants scheme of things:

"When I met him, I immediately knew that Willie was the most open, decent, down-to-earth guy I'd ever seen—completely unspoiled, completely natural. Willie is like another Alabama boy, Joe Louis. He has a gift for doing the right thing at the right time. Willie was one of those good things that just happen once in a while.

"But I was worried to death about the kind of people he might get mixed up with. He'd have to live in Harlem, and believe me, that can be a bad place, full of people just waiting to part an innocent youngster from his money. Somebody had to see to it that Willie wasn't exploited, sift the chalk from the flour, figure out who was in a racket and who was representing a decent organization."

Forbes succeeded exceptionally well, or else Willie wasn't quite as likely to step on a pitfall as Forbes hinted. Forbes set the boy up in an apartment watched over by Mrs. Ann Goosby, who not only saw that the boy ate two big meals at home (breakfast: fruit, bacon, eggs, hashbrown potatoes, milk; supper: steaks or chops and the fixings, with in-between raids on a well-stocked icebox), but also gave forth small motherly tips.

"Not that Willie needed advice too often," Mrs. Goosby has said. "Willie's a good boy. About all I have to lecture him on besides eating properly is his habit of reading comic books. The boy spends hours, I swear it, with those comic books."

Even with this outside counseling and an agency to sift valid ad men from shady operators, Willie Mays did manage to sign his name to a bubble-gum testimonial on an exclusive basis, some weeks after he had already signed an equally exclusive testimonial for the bubble-gum company's chief rival. Something had to be done quickly, and so one day the second gum outfit received this letter:

"Being an infant, and under 21, I could not sign legally with you people. Please forgive me. Willie Mays."

But again, the play's the thing, and it was on the ball field that the 20-year-old infant Willie Mays won his rookie-of-the-year award in 1951. He had to win it under boiler-room pressures, not all of them on the surface. There was the needling a young ballplayer must stand up to, and in Mays' case this meant Roy

Campanella, who had once tried to see the boy signed as a Dodger.

When Mays stepped in to bat one day against Preacher Roe, Campanella began his usual probing needle. He started to fire questions at the boy who was having trouble enough trying to sift the spit from the ball in Roe's hand. As Campy recalls in his book, *It's Good To Be Alive,* Willie was so busy answering, "Yes, Mr. Campanella," or "No, Mr. Campanella," that he was hitting practically nothing against the Dodgers.

Finally, Preacher Roe hosed up his pitch, a ball that flew one way while a heavy spray flew another, and the nonplussed Mays stared in awe and wiped his eye.

"Think he's a good pitcher, eh, Willie?" ribbed Campanella.

"Pretty fair," admitted Mays.

"Well," said Campy pleasantly, "wait till you see Newcombe. He just hates young Negroes," except, of course, Campanella didn't say "Negroes."

Mays reported this and other bits of riding by Campanella (it had all been in what passes for fun in baseball circles) and Durocher bawled the boy out for listening. When he took his next stance against the Dodgers and Campanella opened verbal fire, Willie shook his head and said: "You let me be, Campy. Mr. Durocher says I ain't supposed to talk to you."

And no matter how hard Campy tried ("Willie, you married yet?" and "Willie, are you mad at me?" were his two favorites), Mays kept his mouth shut.

Soon he had stopped hitting "practically nothing," and instead was hitting practically everything against Brooklyn.

As a matter of fact, from 1954 (Mays' first full year) through 1960, Mays batted the exact equivalent of a full season against the Dodgers: 153 games, 587 times at bat. In those 587 at-bats, facing the better and sometimes the wetter pitchers in the league, Mays made 221 hits including 57 home runs, for an overall average of .376. In 1958 alone, Mays hit .483 against the Dodgers.

So Mays lived through the needling; today there's very little directed at him. He also lived through that time in 1951 when he failed to touch third base on an inside-the-park "home run" off Robin Roberts, and the Giants lost a ball game they stood an outside chance of retrieving.

There were, too, the numerous slumps, the occasional lapses on the bases, the strike-outs (in a June ball game Mays struck out three times in a row), the over-eager throwing, the ball-hogging.

But they had to be overshadowed. During one stretch at the end of July and beginning of August, just prior to the Giants' move, Mays couldn't hit anything except home runs. Of six hits, spread over several games, all were home runs.

Most important, as Drebinger had said that very first night, it was the Mays' presence that was more vital than any of his tangible virtues—his homerun bat, his catches, his throws, his speed. The club was infused with the spirit of Mays; the Mays story at the season's end was the Giants' story: the two were one.

I remember making one of the few baseball bets of my life on the day the Giants' 16-game winning streak had come to an end—Howie Pollet shut out New York, 2-0, and a Dodger fan I knew snapped, "I bet they don't play .500 ball the rest of the way."

I understood the reasoning behind his bet, of course. The momentum had ended; now the backlash ought to set in. But I decided to be a sport, and I bet that the Giants would indeed play at least .500 ball the last 28 games. They won 21 and lost 7, for an awesome .750. It was the easiest half-dollar I ever won.

Once again the Giants were the rollicking killers of old, class and spirit combined. Take the game of September 1, the Giants against the Dodgers, Sal Maglie beating Brooklyn for his 18th win of the season and the team making a triple play in the bargain. Don Mueller, a punch-and-poke hitter, hammered two home runs and just before he came to bat for his third trip, the Giant bench received news that Mueller had become a father. So Mueller went out and hit another home run that day, and two more the next, and the Dodgers—about whom it had been wondered aloud whether they'd clinch the pennant earlier than any other winner—had been crushed 8-1 and 11-2. In the two-game set Mays chipped in with four hits.

And there was Bobby Thomson at third base, a position he had played at Jersey City for a spell and at brief intervals with the Giants, but he wasn't a third-baseman and would later, with other ball clubs, be an outfielder again. In a late September game with the Dodgers—always the big ones seemed to be with the Dodgers, although all were big ones—Thomson made a double play at third that one New York newspaperman thought was the best infielding play he'd ever seen.

The Giants were leading, 2-1, behind Sal Maglie, last of the eighth, one out, Jackie Robinson on third and Andy Pafko up. Robinson took his long lead—one step too many, it turned out, and maybe that one step was the pennant—and Pafko hit Maglie's pitch viciously down the third-base line, headed for the left-field corner and two-base hit territory.

But Thomson, leaning his left arm and gloved hand across his body, backhanded the ball on the first short hop; then he swept out his arm, with the ball in his glove, tagged Robinson sliding back into third, straightened up as he transferred the ball from glove to bare hand, and threw out Pafko at first, for the inning-ending double play. When the game was over, and the Giants had won, Leo Durocher began to vomit and couldn't stop.

Down the stretch—or was it retch?—they roared, ignited by Monte Irvin's hitting, Dark's hitting, Thomson's play, Maglie's and Jansen's pitching and Westrum's catching, steadied by Dark and Stanky's work around second, by Lockman's daily improvement at first (in the beginning he didn't know which foot to use on the bag, and pop flies were a source of puzzlement), by Mueller's stroked base hits to all fields—but inspired mainly by the presence of Willie Mays. How else did it happen?

The last days of the season found Brooklyn in

Philadelphia, the Giants in Boston and civilized America at its radios. Jansen beat Spahn and the Phils toyed with the Dodgers—for eight innings. Explosively, the Dodgers came all the way back on a great sprawling money catch by Jackie Robinson, and then they won it in the 14th inning when Robinson hit a home run.

Next, the play-off, and the Giants so brazen, the spirit infected Horace Stoneham. A coin was tossed to determine where the games would be played. The first game would be at one park, and the next two at the other, if a third game would be needed. Stoneham won the toss, and instead of playing it safe, shooting for an opening-day win at the friendly Polo Grounds, he chose to play in Ebbets Field in front of the most fanatic audience in America, and then come home to finish up on Giant home grounds for the last one or two.

You know the rest. Perhaps you even saw it. I was at my desk, and there was the inevitable radio. Said Russ Hodges, a slender second after Bobby Thomson had swung at Ralph Branca's second pitch, a fast ball on his fists:

"There's a drive to left field. Pafko goes back ... It's in the stands for a home run. *I do not believe it! I do not believe it!*" I didn't believe it, either, for a thin moment; my heart stopped for a full beat and then burst full and hot in my throat and ears.

Willie Mays says he didn't believe it either. He had been on deck, waiting to hit, one out, two on, and the Giants trailing by two. Even after the ball had landed in the seats, even after Thomson had begun his slow dancing joy about the bases, Mays still didn't believe it and still didn't move from the on-deck circle, next man up. Then he saw the Dodgers walking off the field, Ralph Branca's big number 13 trudging despondently, headed for the centerfield dressing-room where Branca would finally sit, head down, and cry. Then Mays believed it.

All the years since, I have wondered what would have happened had Thomson made out and Mays had stepped up, two out now, tying runs on. If he had not come through, what would have happened to the legend that has helped make Mays what he is today? What would have happened to the myth that Mays was the lucky piece, the talisman—that with Mays, the Giants win and without him they lose? I have been forced to conclude that had he failed then, it wouldn't have mattered much. The quicksilver still would have broken loose on other grass, a later day, a different game, and Mays would have been the same.

Chapter Six

Willie Mays was 121 games old as a major leaguer when the ball Bobby Thomson hit dipped into the lower deck in left field and Ralph Branca began to cry. In those 121 games Mays batted a neat, not gaudy, .274. Among his 127 hits were 20 home runs, more home runs than a first-year Giant had ever hit. (Orlando Cepeda would later hit 25 home runs in his freshman year, 1958.) Mays also had 22 doubles and five triples. He drove in 68 runs and stole seven bases.

On the face of it, you would call it an impressive performance for a first-year man and let it go at that. Yet it was so much more. It had to be, or why all the fuss, even conceding that a win-starved town was just waiting for something to cheer about? Whenever the team came back, Durocher, Garry Schumacher, or a Giant coach would collar anyone at hand and wave the Mays dossier in front of his nose: a catch by Mays on a ball Rocky Nelson hit in Pittsburgh; a base he stole in Cincinnati (after falling down); a three-run home run in Chicago to win a game in the tenth; a ten-game hitting streak, with four home runs and 16 runs batted in.

Back home, you could see it all yourself. The first week in June, Mays hit a ball off Pittsburgh, left-handed Paul LaPalme that landed in the Giant bullpen on the fly, 440 feet away. A couple days later Mays had two doubles, the second leading to his scoring the game's only run, while Dave Koslo pitched a two-hitter.

The same month he hit a home run in the ninth inning to tie up a game against Philadelphia, and the Giants went on to win. That was starting to be a symbol: the Giants' coming from behind to tie it up and then not blowing it. Durocher said, "Willie has a contagious happiness," and the Giants caught the wonderful sickness, transmuting it into winning games. In a single ball game in July the Giants hit two bases-loaded home runs. And who were the home-run hitters? Catcher Wes Westrum and utility second-baseman Davey Williams, probably the weakest hitters on the entire non-pitching roster. Don Mueller went on a 19-game hitting streak, the longest any Giant would amass until August, 1954, when Mays came back from the Army and wasn't shut out for 21 games.

There was the game of September 29, the day Maglie beat the Braves up in Boston to clinch at least a tie for the Giants on the next-to-last day of the 154-game schedule. Mays didn't hit, but in the second inning he walked. He stole second and third, then scored on a short single by Mueller for the game's first run, the only run needed in a 3-0 win.

That 1951 season was dotted by Mays' deeds; you had to notice him. The Giants hadn't had anyone quite like Mays since Blondy Ryan, back in 1933, whose famous, "They-can't-beat-us!" telegram to his teammates is supposed to have lifted the briefly-faltering pennant-bound Giants. Ryan had few skills of any great note; he played a flashy, erratic short-stop, but like Mays he often came up with the big play. Moreover, he had the knack of inspiring his teammates just by his presence. Mays had this same inspirational quality, multiplied by a half-dozen skills beyond the shortstop's limited resources.

The fans knew it, too. On August 17, 1951—Mays was less than three months a major leaguer—a delegation came up from Trenton to honor the centerfielder in one of those dreary pre-game ceremonies which ought to be abolished by national referendum. (The main gift was a huge oil painting of Mays.) And on September 1, 1951, the bleacher fans anted up enough money to buy Mays a watch.

There is nothing surprising about these gestures, except that they occurred so early. Mays' infancy, legally speaking, would not end until May, 1952. I do not recall that Pete Reiser, who surely had a far more spectacular first year than had Mays, was honored in his rookie season. Mickey Mantle played 2,000 ball games before he was so honored.

Perhaps it was Mays' ability to transmit his enthusiasm, his *joie de jouer*, that made such an impact. The press was alert to this facet of Mays, and we soon began to read how Mays would leave the Polo Grounds after a day game and head into Harlem to play a little pick-up basketball in a school yard, or swat rubber balls with a broomstick with the neighborhood kids. (Actually, the great reams of stickball publicity were still in the offing; it was not until 1954 that the public was made fully aware of Mays the stickball player, although he played about as much in 1951 as he did in 1954.)

From Mays' teammates came further evidence of his near-childlike approach to life. Monte Irvin used to tell how Willie was always trying to get him to accompany Willie to another drug store for another ice cream soda. "Sometimes he'd drink five or six sodas in an afternoon," Irvin used to marvel. Irvin also told how Willie had once before been honored in a pre-game ceremony. Back in Birmingham, when Willie was eighteen or so, the fans had got together and bought him a brand new Mercury. Willie had driven it to the gas station and nonchalantly asked the attendant for $25-worth of gas.

Willie used to like to go around poking his finger in Giant teammates' ears. If Irvin slept too long to suit him, Willie would either turn his record player to full volume or throw ice water in Monte's face. Mays liked to wrestle with Monte, horseplay-style. Irvin was two inches taller than Mays, and fifteen or twenty pounds heavier (he is still built like a Mr. America), but Irvin complained once that it was like "tangling with a tiger."

And always there were tales of girls chasing Willie: phone calls at the clubhouse, girls outside the park, and Frank Forbes busy sifting.

So a nearly complete picture of the young Willie Mays started to emerge: talented almost beyond description, colorful, acclaimed almost beyond reason, and adolescent. Boyish, actually. He had little use for certain men's ways. After the Giants clinched the

1951 pennant in the hysterical play-off with the Dodgers, the champagne corks popped, and Hank Thomson insised that Willie try at least one tiny sip. Reluctantly, Mays took a sip. Almost immediately he became violently ill. (Three years later, after the 1954 pennant had been won, Hank Thomson again proffered Mays a single swallow of champagne, and again Mays became ill. "You are obviously maturing," Hank Thomson said; "took you two more minutes this time.")

With the champagne bout of 1951, the season did not end. There was still the World Series, against a good, nearly great Yankee club. As expected, the Yankees won a six-game set, after the Giants had won two of the first three. The way the Yankees won was not quite as expected. The Yankees beat Giant aces Larry Jansen and Sal Maglie and lost to Koslo and Jim Hearn. According to the great American indoor game of "If," the Giants would have taken the Series to seven games, with Maglie or Hearn ready to pitch the decider, had the usually reliable Monte Irvin handled a long drive in the final game by Hank Bauer. Irvin backtracked on the ball instead of turning and running for it (left field at Yankee Stadium is the trickiest outfield post in the majors), and the ball landed behind him for a three-run triple. The Giants lost, 4-3. You can't knock Irvin. He hit .458 in the Series, with eleven hits (a record for a six-game set), and in the first inning of the first game stole home, something nobody had done in a Series since 1928.

The Giants were hurt by the loss of Don Mueller,

who in the ninth inning of that heroic last play-off had injured an ankle sliding into third and had been carried off on a stretcher. Hank Thompson, a utility infielder at the time, played right field in the Series and hit a feeble .143.

With Irvin, Mays, and Thompson, it was the first all-Negro outfield in major-league history.

Mays himself offered little help, grounding into his record-making three double plays in the fourth game and contributing just four singles in twenty-two at-bats, for .182. He drove in one run. The first two games were at the Stadium, for Mays a strange field with strange fans (70,000 the first day). Such newness has often served to upset Mays. Moreover, a dose of good old-fashioned Yankee pitching—Allie Reynolds, Ed Lopat, and Vic Raschi were the three starters— may well have throttled a still-young ballplayer who had been, after all, just a .274 hitter in his league.

The Series loss didn't matter much (to a Giant fan, the 1951 pennant run was the big story; in 1954, naturally, the Series was the story; in 1962, again the heartclutching pennant play-off was what counted— feel free to call this hypocrisy), except that it paid the Yankees $1500 more per man than it did the Giants. Each Yankee took home $6,446.09, each Giant $4,951.03. But most important, the year had been a great one for Mays and the club; the thirteen-year drought had finally ended.

Waiting for Mays in Alabama was an October date with his local draft board. The United States was still embroiled in violent "peace action" in Korea, not unlike later fighting in Vietnam, and Willie Mays, at twenty, appeared to be a most logical candidate for induction. There were two complications.

Ever since the Barons began to pay Mays for playing baseball, part of his salary had gone to help his numerous brothers and sisters by his mother's second marriage. He turned over another portion of his income to his Aunt Sarah. As Mays moved up baseball's pay ladder from Birmingham through Trenton and Minneapolis to New York, the money he was able to send home increased, until in 1951 he was more or less supporting his family. His mother's second husband, Frank McMorris, was a plumber's helper, earning around $50 a week, not enough to bring up that many kids comfortably. Accordingly, Willie applied for a 3-A classification: "registrant deferred by reason of extreme hardship to dependents." The application was rejected by Mays' board.

Mays had probably reached that point of national attention at which there are disadvantages. Had he been anybody else earning $5,500 a year (not counting the World Series), with so many half-brothers and half-sisters, it is likely that the draft board would have deferred him. But Mays was a ballplayer, a man who put in approximately four hours' work each day, and then for only six months of the year. He was a ballplayer who everybody knew drank five or six ice-cream sodas at a sitting and liked to buy clothes. He was a man—we all knew—without a single care in the world.

It was a question, then, of drafting Willie despite strong grounds for deferment, or not drafting him and facing an outraged public, already suspicious of athletes with punctured ear drums or flat feet—apparently not strong enough to pick up cigarette butts, but healthy enough to up-end a 200-pound catcher at home plate, or out-wrestle husky Monte Irvin.

The argument was put forward that before Mays had begun to contribute heavily, all those kids had somehow been taken care of. Without Mays the situation would not be good, but it wouldn't be disastrous, because part of his monthly Army pay would go home, plus a bit from the federal government to help the family subsist.

Hence Mays was called up. And he promptly failed his Army Government Classification Test.

The AGCT, a kind of intelligence test, presents vocabulary questions, mathematical problems, general information queries. Like most intelligence tests it tests not intelligence, but verbal ability. A graduate of a general academic high school program usually does well on such a test, but Mays was an industrial student. Such tests are discriminating also insofar as questions often employ terms most familiar to the upper-middle class. Besides, Mays has never pretended to be a fluent man, though he is very far from a stupid man.

Whatever the reason for his low score on the AGCT, it aroused an already curious public. So Mays took the test over again—as did Cassius Clay recently—and this time passed it. A date with Uncle Sam was finally set for May, 1952. (Most ballplayers now get out of long stretches of military service by signing for reserve duty and breaking up their training into six-month periods every fall and winter, until they have fulfilled their obligation.)

That Willie knew he'd be leaving soon for nearly two years of sevice may have blunted the keen edge of his enthusiasm in the brief 1952 season. In 34 games with the Giants, Willie batted an anemic .236, his poorest showing for any single season. Knowing what we do of Mays' occasional month-long slumps, it wouldn't have surprised anybody if he had hit a healthy .320 or thereabouts over the full season. There were in fact days when he looked like the greatest player in the game. In a ball game against the Pirates early that season I saw him drive two enormous triples over the Pirate centerfielder's head, and the only argument in the bleachers that day was whether Mays had actually got good wood on the ball. Still, days like this had to be few in a .236 month.

There may have been another reason for Mays' depression. On April 2, near the end of spring training, the Giants faced the Cleveland Indians in a Denver ball game on a cold, gray day. It was the fifth inning, and Monte Irvin, having coaxed a walk from Bob Lemon, was on first base. Mays drove a line single to center and Irvin wheeled past second on his way to third. Pete Reiser was the Indian centerfielder, the other really great natural ballplayer of the postwar period and one of the fastest men any of us ever saw in baseball clothes. He quickly calculated the speed of the men on base. He knew he would not nail Irvin who also could run like the wind (and who was doing so for the very last time in his life) at third; he knew if he threw to second base, Mays would be driven back to first after the long wide turn; and he knew finally (this is how fast a great player's mind works) that if he threw *toward* third, shortstop Ray Boone would be able to cut off the throw and cut down Mays if Willie tried to advance on Reiser's throw. This last is what happened.

When Irvin heard the ball spatter into Boone's glove, he knew there'd be no play at third and tried to hold up his slide. Irvin's body was driving for third, legs pumping, toes digging, when his mind dictated a sudden slowdown. It didn't work. It seldom does. Ask Tommy Davis, to whom the same thing happened in 1965.

Irvin's spikes caught and his body, unchecked, pinwheeled over the leg and flipped Irvin onto his face. The right ankle was broken so badly that the foot dangled at a nearly 90-degree angle to the rest of the leg. Trainer Doc Bowman held the ankle bones, so that the splinters would do no more damage to nerves and muscles.

Mays, out at second on Boone's flip to the bag, lay sprawled on his face, beating his hands against the dirt. He knew by the sound and by Irvin's scream what had happened to his teammate, his roommate, his friend, and the Giants' chances. Mays cried out, "Why did I have to get a hit, why did I have to get a hit?" He lay there and wept, and an ambulance finally and delicately carted Irvin off. Leo Durocher came out of the dugout, the crack of bone still echoing in the Denver air, and after he'd taken one look, he went back to the bench, gray and sick. Coach Herman Franks—later to manage the Giants—had held up his hands to let Irvin know there would be no play at third. Now he turned away in nausea.

There is no way of saying how much all this affected young Willie Mays, who was closer to Irvin than to anybody on the club, with the exception of Durocher, and the Durocher relationship was a far different thing. Monte Irvin was like an older, steadying brother to Mays. Today it is Monte Irvin who suggests in print that Willie Mays is now mature enough to manage a big-league baseball team.

But this was a young Mays, not yet old enough to vote. He was shattered nearly as badly as Irvin's bone and never again revived completely that brief season, despite his two-triple afternoon. His .236 average, his four home runs, his 23 runs-batted-in may all be products of that grim day in Denver.

This makes the next fact even more startling. When Mays left for the Army on May 28, 1952, the Giants were leading the National League by two-and-a-half games. In the 34 games Mays had played, the Giants had won 27 and lost seven.

With Mays gone, the Giants promptly lost eight of their next ten, dropped out of the league lead, and ended the year in second place, four-and-a-half games behind the Dodgers. Dodger manager Charley Dressen crowed happily if ungrammatically, "The Giants is dead! The Giants is dead!"

The 1952 Giant record is a remarkable one, considering the loss of both Mays and Irvin. Irvin, though badly slowed down, managed to get back into action in August. In 46 games, appearing mainly as a pinch-hitter, he drove in 21 runs, as opposed to his 1951 total of exactly 100 runs more.

So it might be argued (and it was) that Mays alone didn't cause this failure to win in 1952. But in 1953, with Mays gone all year and Irvin playing 124 games and hitting .329 (though considerably slower than in his prime), the Giants sank to fifth place with a 70-won, 84-lost record, 35 games behind Brooklyn.

In 1954 Mays was back. So were the Giants.

Chapter Seven

There may have been softer Army tours of duty in those days than Willie Mays' but surely not too many. He was in service from May 29, 1952, until March 2, 1954. In those 640 days, nearly all spent at Fort Eustis, Virginia, Mays engaged in approximately 180 baseball games. When he wasn't playing baseball, he went down to the gym and played basketball. And when he was doing neither (which wasn't often), he performed calisthenics, sometimes leading a platoon of GI's in nip-ups.

Mays was officially assigned to a transportation unit, which occasionally gave him a chance to drive around a little—an activity Mays enjoys almost as much as batting practice.

They had a pretty good team at Eustis, including a pitcher named Vernon Law. Red Sox outfielder Karl Olson and a Piedmont League second-baseman were two of Mays' teammates. Sometimes the Eustis boys would suit up to meet another good service team from nearby Fort Meyer, Virginia. Mays would then bat against a young fireballer named Johnny Antonelli, a bonus baby out of Boston Brave uniform, whose equally arduous Army life would see him wind up with 42 wins, 20 of them consecutive. Antonelli went overseas and picked up two shut-out wins in Japan.

It is unfair to single out Mays or Antonelli. During World War II, when the need for able-bodied men was far more urgent, the only digging that many inducted professional baseballers did was to get a better grip in the batter's box with spiked shoes provided by the service quartermaster.

The Army did more than keep Mays in condition; it actually improved him. The calisthenics built up his upper arms until they are today a pair of the more awesome sights this side of Randy Matson. Vin Scully says of Mays, "When you first see him in uniform and read his physical statistics, he does not impress you as a terribly big man. But when you see him with his shirt off, he looks like the heavyweight champion of the world." Mays has a magnificently muscled upper torso, upper arms, shoulders, and chest. He would undoubtedly have had such a torso even without Army exercises, but Fort Eustis hurried it along.

And so Willie enjoyed himself getting bigger-armed and stronger and playing baseball as though that were the reason he'd been drafted. One day, with Eustis leading 14-0, he stole third, and Mays said, when word reached Leo Durocher, sick enough with the '53 Giants as it was, "I hear Leo like to go wild." The picture of Mays' risking injury on the basketball court and baseball diamonds must have haunted Durocher's sleep. In fact, Mays once did plow into third base and suffer a slight fracture of his ankle.

The most important thing Mays picked up at Fort

Eustis, besides strawberry bruises from sliding, was his now-famous basket catch. Charles Einstein, speaking for Mays is Willie's autobiography, explains the thinking behind the evolution of the basket catch.

"Most outfielders make their throws from the back-of-the-ear throwing position. Most of my throws, though, are made from lower down and farther out from the body, tending toward the sidearm. It occurred to me I could save a fraction of time by catching the ball lower down, too."

Thus evolved the basket, or bread-basket, or belt-buckle catch, where Mays holds his glove at his waist, pounds it once or twice or thrice in a habit that now tells viewers he has zeroed in on the ball, and then makes the catch with thumbs out and palms up. The usual outfield catch has the glove at shoulder or in front of the man's face, thumbs in. Mays is not the inventor of the catch, although like most great scientists he probably reached the idea independently. Rabbit Maranville had been bread-basketing major-league pop flys at shortstop for 18 years when Mays was born, and continued to eat them up for another four more seasons. Bill Rigney also caught infield fly balls that way when he played second, short, or third for the Giants. Mays was a grade-schooler at the time. There have been others. Today Bob Clemente, a splendid fly-catcher, makes his plays at the belt buckle, and he insists he was catching baseballs that way before he ever saw Willie Mays.

Grabbing fly balls at the waist, Mays no longer had to bring the ball down and back to let loose a throw. The ball was already down. Mays always threw with great power, velocity, and accuracy. Now he had the extra advantage of ridding himself of the ball more quickly. Runners these days advance on Mays only when the odds are strongly in their favor. In 1965, their late-summer winning streak just under way, the Giants moved into Los Angles for a two-game series on September 6 and 7. The Dodgers led the league by two games, but they had played a few more games than the Giants. A Giant sweep would put San Francisco in the lead. In the Dodger half of the first inning, Maury Wills opened with a triple to deep right-center. Then Jim Gilliam drove a long fly ball to centerfield, where Mays tapped his big pocket three times and made the catch.

Wills started for the plate. No need to tell you of Wills, of course. You know his speed. And this was not a shallow fly. It had been hit to straightaway dead center. Mays had no opportunity to run back and then charge forward for the catch, to put extra momentum on his throw. He had to catch it in his tracks. Yet Wills just beat the astonishing throw, sliding under Tom Haller's lunging tag. It appeared from the press box that had Haller blocked the plate more aggressively, Wills would have been out. Still, safe or out, the throw drew a long gasp from the pro-Dodger audience. Then there was silence, then a great roar. What made the closeness of the play possible was not actually the magnificent throw. It was the style of the throwing. There was Mays making the catch, and with his famous sleight-of-hand the ball was plucked out of the glove, swept to the side and shot forward. No face-high catch with its necessary long reverse-and-down action before the ball could be projected, no long windup was necessary. Mays' belt-buckle catch had been put on display and proved to be far more than a gimmick or showboating gesture.

At the same time in service that Mays was toying with the new catch, he also perfected a first-baseman's use of his fielder's glove, enabling him to keep his hand and fingers in the heel of the glove, leaving the rest—and greater portion—of the glove fingerless. Because Mays' hand is so big, he is able to control his glove even though most of it is empty. "The pocket," Mays says, "where the ball hits doesn't have any of me in it at all."

The purpose, then, it not merely to add inches of reach, but to keep his fingers from messing up the catch. One day in 1958 the Giants returned to California after blowing an early summer lead, and the pressure was now off with the realization that the Giants could not win the pennant. Bill Rigney, a happier warrior in those days than he would be in 1959 and 1960, was talking about a meeting between Mays and Tris Speaker.

It was one of those moments in history that should have been preserved by a tape recorder and a movie camera. You know, like John L. Sullivan meeting with Muhammad Ali, or Andrew Jackson with Lyndon Johnson, or Mark Antony with Liz Taylor, had any of these been possible. Speaker and Mays have long been considered two of the greatest, if not *the* greatest defensive outfielders the game has known. And here they were, chatting together, swapping trade secrets.

Mays, who had never seen Speaker in action, explained to him all about the basket catch and the extra inches of reach. Then, according to Rigney, he demonstrated for Speaker how a third factor had just naturally grown out of the other two. Mays caught a fly ball at his waist, thumbs out, glove facing straight up, the ball nestling in the fingerless pocket. He then snatched the ball from his glove with his right hand, preparing to throw.

"See?" Mays lectured Speaker; "when I grab the ball that way, with my right hand, I never get mixed up with the fingers of my left hand. They ain't there." "He actually taught Speaker something," Manager Rigney said. It may not have taught Speaker anything at all, except that baseball gloves are much bigger today than they used to be, but it was apparently Mays who did the talking.

When Willie got out of the Army March 2, 1954, with his basket catch and an almost unswerving beyond-the-call devotion to baseball, Frank Forbes was waiting for him at the Fort Eustis separation center. He hustled Mays to the Washington, D.C. airport. The weather was so cold that Forbes peeled off his overcoat and huddled Mays inside it. Now Forbes is a *very* big man, and the coat fitted Mays almost as badly as humility does Joe Namath. To make matters worse, Forbes slid layers of newspapers inside his shirt, in the hobo's old trick of keeping warm, and these two refugees from Goodwill hurried to catch a plane for Phoenix. On any other day, they might have not attracted so much nervous attention, but the day before, four Puerto Ricans had shot up the House of

Representatives, wounding five Congressmen. The sight of two dark-skinned men, one whose shirt bulged and crackled suspiciously and the other in a coat three sizes too big, was as unsettling as a Mafia mobster carrying a violin case. Washington must have been relieved to see Mays and Forbes fly off.

Washington's relief was nothing compared to the Giant's pleasure at seeing them arrive in Phoenix.

Mays changed into his uniform and, with photographers lined up, twisted his way through the tunnel that led to the dugout on the third-base side of Phoenix's now outdated Municipal Stadium. As a grinning Mays trotted out of the tunnel, flashbulbs popped and a Giant official said, "There's the pennant." Durocher bearhugged his centerfielder and declared, "Here's the key to the pennant." Then Mays hit a ball over the fence in his first trip up. Leo Durocher, basking in self-importance and reflected glory, said to his audience of newsmen,

"Willie must have been born under some kind of star. The stage always seems set for him to do something dramatic."

The Durocher remark caught that breathless, mercurial, about-to-explode quality and nicely stamped it into print.

Willie Mays was back and Durocher had him.

After the first game of March 2, there were more interviews, conducted in chatter-gun style because the enthusiasm of 1951 was as vivid as ever. Bill Roeder of the New York *World-Telegram and Sun,* worded it perfectly: "Willie answers all your questions breath-

97

lessly. He sounds like a guy who has just been told that his house is on fire."

One reporter asked Willie, "How much money you going to ask for?" and Mays, young as he was, knew when to demur.

The reporter persisted: "You going to ask for $25,-000, Willie?"

"You crazy, man? If I ask for that kind of money, that man take a gun and shoot me." So Mays signed for $13,000, a few thousand over his 1952 pay, but still the biggest bargain since the Staten Island ferry ride.

What exactly were the Giants buying, for $13,000, in 1954? This Willie Mays was just a trifle bigger than the old Mays; the scales said three pounds at the official weigh-in. One hundred and eighty-five. It is just about the weight Mays now carries in the field at mid-season.

So the Mays of today and the Mays of 1951 and of 1954 are pretty much the same man, in size. But in 1954, before the season started, there was still a question about the young man (no longer a boy, now that he was going on 23) that had not been answered. Al Lopez, manager of the Indians, watched Mays closely that spring practice session, watched him whistle out his line drives and boom his soaring parabolas over the fences. Lopez noticed how infielders played Mays backed up and pulled deeply to the left. He said slowly and shrewdly and only after he had taken time to study the Giant, "Mays is a .270 hitter who might hit .300 if they teach him to bunt down the third-base line."

Chapter Eight

One day early in the 1954 season Willie Mays did bunt. There were runners on first and second and none out. Mays tried to bunt down the third-base line to move them up, but instead tapped the ball straight back to the pitcher who threw to third for a force out.

A newsman cackled, "Ah! They have at last found Willie Mays's weakness. He can't bunt." (When in the World Series of 1954, with two out and an Indian on third, Willie Mays caught a fly ball—for the third out—and made a tremendous throw to the plate, a newsman cracked, "Ah! They have at last found Willie Mays' weakness. He can't count.!")

In 1954, Mays could do everything else.

"Spectacularly routine," a reporter yawned, over a Mays catch.

A St. Louis newsman one day saw a glint of metal on the grass out in centerfield, near Mays. "Look," he said sourly, "Willie Mays' halo fell off."

One day Mays raced to his left for a gloved-hand grab of a line drive. His hat flew off just as he caught the ball, so he swung around and caught his hat with his right hand before it touched the ground. "That's not fair," an onlooker grunted. "He used two hands."

Ethel Barrymore said in an interview on her 75th

birthday, "Isn't Willie Mays wonderful?" If the remark seems irrelevant, you must remember that this was the wonderful summer of '54.

The *New York Times Book Review* section had a similar comment: "Topic A is either the hydrogen bomb, sex, where-shall-I-go-on-my-vacation, or Willie Mays."

Here is a quick run-down on what Mays did in 1954, crystallized into those dull statistics which never tell the whole story.

In 1954 Mays hit .345, to lead both leagues. He hit 41 home runs and drove in 110 runs. It was the first time in over 30 years that the National League's leading hitter for average had also hit over 40 home runs. Mays had 33 doubles and 13 triples (this was the first time he broke Mel Ott's all-time record of 81 extra-base hits), and the collection of long hits in 1954 gave Mays a slugging percentage of .667. You figure slugging percentage by dividing times at bat into a man's total bases (one base for a single, two for a double, and so on). Mays has led his league in slugging five times.

In the field, Mays had 14 assists and participated in eight double plays—phenomenal figures, especially so for a man whose arm terrorized the league's runners into staying put. If you do not realize how really remarkable is an outfielder's participation in eight double plays, may I refer you to the poem by that old Giant fan, Franklin P. Adams, which immortalized the old Chicago Cub double-play team of Joe Tinker, Johnny Evers, and Frank Chance. The poem begins:

These are the saddest of possible words,
Tinker-to-Evers-to-Chance. . . .

FPA's poem appeared in 1908. In 1908 the Tinker-to-Evers-to-Chance (or short to second to first) combination accounted for eight double plays, the same number Willie Mays was involved in, out there in centerfield.

In one weekend Willie Mays appeared on three network television shows. The same month, he was on 15 other radio and television programs. His life was portrayed in serial form in two newspapers—memoirs, at the age of 23!—and was carried by a national wire service.

Hot-dog packages, bubble-gum packages (just one company, thank you!), and chewing tobacco (though Willie doesn't chew) all carried Willie Mays baseball cards, together with those of other stars. By the time the season had ended, a Willie Mays card was worth two Duke Sniders or three Mickey Mantles on the Gum Exchange.

Willie Mays soon was saying to newsmen, "If you haven't seen my agent, I'm not going to talk to you." There was a $500 fee for television and radio appearances; later that year it reached $1,000. Merchandising tie-ins brought Mays another thousand per.

When the Giants took time off to engage in an exhibition game with their farm team, the Minneapolis Millers (and lost, 6-5), Minneapolis fans stood patiently in line the entire night before to buy tickets. Willie Mays would be coming home! You can measure your hero by the number of towns that claim him as their own.

When Willie Mays peeled off his uniform in the Giant clubhouse on Eighth Avenue north of 155th Street and in civvies played a little stickball on St.

Nicholas Place in Harlem, newsmen and photographers were on hand to record the incongruous sight of a national figure fooling around with 15- and 16-year-old kids. Six national magazines ran stories on Mays' stickball.

A word here about the stickball legend. I am an old stickball player. It is not much of a sport. You can play it in a big playground, where there is some room to make a catch, but you can't play it easily on a narrow city street. The advantage is all the hitter's. No fielding is possible in street games, and that is probably why it attracted Willie Mays. He didn't *play* stickball; he took batting practice.

One sixteen-year-old let the truth out: "Willie's a con man," the boy said; "he tells us kids we'll get our turn to hit, but we never do."

What it came to was Willie Mays' grabbing a broomstick and asking some kid to bounce in a few pitches. In stickball distance is measured by the number of manhole covers the drive passes. The manhole covers on St. Nicholas Place at 155th Street are spaced about 30 yards apart, so a three-sewer shot is some 270 feet, or just far enough to make the foul poles for home runs at the Polo Grounds. There are rumors that Willie sometimes hit the rubber ball five sewers.

Even if Willie was conning the kids, he still enjoyed their company. He would come around to shoot baskets, or have a hardball catch if ball and gloves were available, or a rubber-ball catch if not. "Somebody's got to teach these kids right," Mays would explain. Then he would round up the neighborhood for ice-cream sodas, until Mrs. Ann Goosby stuck her head out the window and yelled Willie home for supper.

It was as if Mays, the professional star with a salary of $13,000, were wistfully capturing a moment of play for playing's sake alone. Mays actually entered professional baseball too soon. He was playing for the Barons before he finished high school. Even before that, at the age of fourteen, he was getting a few dollars to play semi-pro ball.

Monte Irvin used to draw Mays aside and explain soberly, "You lose your batting eye, playing stickball," and Mays argued back. It wasn't a case of losing or not losing his eye; it was a plea to be allowed to have fun.

Willie Mays grabbed his fun, bubbling and contagious, where he could. After the 1954 All-Star game Charley Grimm said, "Willie Mays is the only ballplayer who can help a team just by riding on the bus with it."

But even with the lingering traces of youth, 1954 marked the coming of baseball age for Willie Mays. No ballplayer had a greater year. No athlete had a greater year, even though this was the year that England's Roger Bannister ran the four-minute-mile. When the season ended, Mays was voted the Most Valuable Player in baseball and the Athlete of the Year; he won a diamond-studded belt worth, it is claimed by the Hickok people, $10,000, and was feted by B'nai B'rith. A play he had made in the opening game of the 1954 World Series was acclaimed the sports moment of the year.

But the World Series was far off, and so were the awards, when, in April, a group of us piled onto the 8th Avenue subway train and rode up to the Polo Grounds to find seats in upper left field and watch the Giants open the season with the Dodgers. Carl Erskine faced Sal Maglie, and Mays was back in action for the first time in nearly two years.

In those days Erskine was one of the better pitchers in the league, with a downbreaking curve ball that Leo Durocher used to say dropped right off the table. Pool table, no doubt. Like many other great curveball pitchers, Erskine was also very fast. In later years, when the hitters started to get to Erskine, he still had that wonderful curve ball, but the fast ball had lost its pep. The batters could wait, knowing that Erskine had become a one-pitch pitcher.

But in 1954 Erskine, then 27 years old, was a strong compact right-hander who would win 18 games that season. Two years earlier he had pitched a no-hitter against the Cubs. In 1956 he would pitch another no-hitter, against the Giants. Only two pitchers in the league, Robin Roberts and Harvey Haddis, would strike out more men in '54.

In the seventh inning of that opening game, the score tied, 3-3, Erskine threw a fast ball—very fast—to Willie Mays. Mays teed off with all the gleeful savagery of a free-swinging young man.

The result was awesome. The ball traveled off Mays' bat in a long white blur, a straight line that ended abruptly in the upper deck, above the 414-foot marker. Though Mays says he has hit a ball or two harder and farther, it is difficult to imagine his ever having hit one more fiercely.

With that gigantic line-drive home run, the Giants had won their first ball game of 1954, 4-3. They had beaten the defending champions, the hated Dodgers, in their first head-to-head meeting. This marked Mays' return to baseball.

Early in June, the Giants took over the league lead and were never headed. A fifth-place team that had trailed the winner by 35 games the year before had made up the entire gap to win by five.

You cannot attribute the whole 40-game difference to Mays' return. There was also John Antonelli, winning 21 games, the best pitcher in baseball that year; Mueller, batting over .340; Alvin Dark, playing a great, heady, spirited game at shortstop and hitting well; Davey Williams, handling 261 consecutive chances at second base without an error in midsummer. And the fantastic pinch-hitting! No team had ever hit more than seven pinch home runs in one season. The 1954 Giant bench delivered ten, eight of them directly involved in winning games.

Hoot Evers, an aging outfielder resurrected from the American League, made exactly one hit for the Giants before being waived back to the other league, and the hit was a home run on a two-strike pitch with two out in the bottom of the ninth inning of a tied ball game. Bob Hofman hit three pinch home runs to set a record. His first was a three-run home run in a game the Giants won by two runs. His second was a two-run home run in a game the Giants won by one run. His third was another two-run home run in a game the Giants won again by one.

And then there was Dusty Rhodes. James Lamar Rhodes, named Dusty because Rhodes boys have always been named Dusty, was a southern boy whose father, Dusty said, was a corn farmer. ("He raised 200 gallons.") In a late-June game with the Dodgers, the Giants, trailing by a run in the bottom of the 13th inning, two out, and the bases loaded, Rhodes hit a two-strike pitch into centerfield, and the Giants had won the biggest game of the year. Two days later in a nearly identical spot, Rhodes beat the Dodgers again with another pinch single.

With all this, the feeling persists that Mays was the real difference between the '53 and '54 teams.

When it became apparent that the Giants would clinch the pennant, the Cleveland Indians put a couple of scouts on the New Yorkers to see what could be learned in addition to what had already been ascertained during spring training. (It had been ascertained that Al Lopez was leading the pack in the race for biggest damfool of the year, because of his remark about Mays' hitting .270 unless he learned to bunt.)

The new scouting report on Mays read: "Gets most of his long-ball hits on high pitches. Gets most of his hits on low pitches." It posted a dilemma: throw Mays high, and you might breeze it by, but then again he might hit it out of the park; throw him low, and he won't hit many home runs, but he'll hit.

In 1954 Willie Mays was two hitters. Through the first half and into July, he was a free-wheeling slugger and a long lunging swinger. He lashed his 34-ounce,

35-inch yellow Genuine Mays Louisville Slugger and sent baseballs into the upper deck of sections 36 and 37 of the Polo Grounds, or into the sky and gone in every park he visited. Mays had 31 home runs up to the All-Star break. When he hit his 36th off Tom Poholsky, 447 feet into the upper left-centerfield stands at the Polo Grounds, the date was July 28 and the game was the Giants' 95th of the campaign. (In 1927, the year he hit his Sixty, Babe Ruth did not get his 36th until August 10, in the Yankees' 110th game.)

From that date on, Mays hit just five home runs, two of them inside-the-park jobs. A slump? In a way. Surely a home-run drought. Mays went 17 days between his 36th and 37th. (The Babe Ruth record went back on the mantel, to remain until Roger Maris came along in 1961.) Yet Mays without home runs became a hitting machine: line drives ripped to all fields, depending on where the ball was pitched. In that stretch, Mays hit .379. And it wasn't a case of his trying simply to stroke the ball and settling for singles. Mays filled the daily box scores with doubles and triples, balls lined between the outfielders or pounded over the centerfielder's head.

Yet something had occurred. The change was too dramatic, the falling off of home runs too sudden. The explanation most commonly accepted, that Mays deliberately chose to cut down on his home-run production, to go for any kind of base hit, is based on a brief one-way conversation between Mays and Durocher, as July ran into August and the Giants lost six games in a row and suddenly had to face Brooklyn and Milwaukee challenges.

Durocher said to Mays, "Look, we've been losing and I'm going to bat you fourth. You can raise your average if you start hitting to right field." Mays went on his 21-game streak with almost no home runs. The Giants held off the enemy and won going away.

I think this puts the cart before the horse. When Mays joined the Giants in 1954, he had behind him the equivalent of a single year in the majors. In that year, 1951 and 1952 combined, he had hit .266. A man who hits .266 is obviously doing something wrong, perhaps hitching at the plate or taking his eye off the ball. His stance may be at fault. There must be a pitch or two he is having trouble with.

National League pitchers, a grim, sharp-witted crew of skilled operators who pass the word to each other on the league's different hitters, probably thought, as the 1954 season opened, that they had compiled a pretty good book on Willie Mays. Whatever the book read, it read wrong. Because there was Mays, booming drives out of sight, making his pass at the Ruth record. It takes time for a leagueful of pitchers to rewrite their precious book on opposing hitters. A man doesn't like to admit that his carefully nursed pitch has suddenly stopped doing the job. "Lucky blind stiff," the pitcher mutters; *"I'll* show him." In comes the same delivery. And out it booms again.

But by mid-July the bitter truth had sunk in. Whatever the pitch was, it had to be buried.

I'll wager that the pitch Mays used to see regularly and then stopped seeing almost entirely was a high hard one, on the inside corner. Not just because this is a pitch righthanded sluggers will hit into the left-field seats if they come around on it. Back in Arizona that spring, Cleveland's Ralph Kiner told reporters that he had noticed Mays "laying off the high inside pitch he used to be a sucker for."

Laid off, perhaps, because it was inside, not quite taking the edge of the plate. Mays had disciplined himself enough not to bite at too many pitches that weren't strikes. So the pitchers slowly, automatically and probably unconsciously shifted the pitch just inches over, to grab the inside corner of the plate. Except when they came in that way, Mays leaped on the ball and rode it out of the park.

In late July the pitchers began to aim for the outside corner, began to invite Mays to generate his own power if he wanted home runs. Now Mays began to see a stream of curve balls, a series of low outside pitches. As any batter knows, you are not likely to pull such a pitch—low and away—around and into the left-field seats. Mays stopped his lunging somewhat and started hitting the ball to whatever field seemed called for by the pitch.

It wasn't so much that Mays deliberately shot for right field as that the pitchers practically begged him to hit the ball to right field, or at least away from the left-field foul pole. Part of the conspiracy lies in the way the Polo Grounds was constructed: the short distances to the foul lines were deceiving, because the fences fell away abruptly, and tremendous drives to right and left centerfield, or to dead center, usually ended up in an outfielder's glove. Keep a pull-hitter from pulling in the Polo Grounds, and you throttled his power.

From late July through September Mays began to loop outside pitches to right field and rip slightly right-of-center pitches to right center, center, and left center, depending on the speed of the delivery. On pitches to his inside strength—rarer each day—Mays would pull. By the time the season ended, Mays had the system down pat. On Sunday, September 26, facing Robin Roberts in Philadelphia on the last day of the season, Mays lined an inside pitch to left field for a single. He also hit two of Roberts' outside curves over the head of Richie Ashburn in deep right-center-field for a double and a triple. He had won the batting championship.

On July 22 and 23 the Giants lost ball games to the Braves in Milwaukee. It was the first time in two months that the Giants had lost two games in a row. Willie Mays was not in the lineup. He returned the next day, and the Giants lost four more in a row. You might say: "See, it wasn't Mays, because with Mays in there, they still couldn't win." But you could also say: "See, Mays went out of the lineup and threw the boys so badly it took quite some time to recover."

The six-game losing streak began just after Willie's Aunt Sarah died. When the news reached Mays in St. Louis, he took himself out of a game in the fourth inning and prepared to go to Alabama for the funeral. He then learned that the funeral would not be until later in the week, so he went to Cincinnati for a double-header. When the Giants moved to Milwaukee, Mays went home, and Rhodes and Whitey Lock-

man played centerfield for three days, the Giants
winning the first and losing the next two.

Mays was badly shaken by his aunt's death. He
went back with Frank Forbes and sat alone in a
room in his aunt's house and mourned this woman
who had been nearly a mother to him.

Yet her death did not appear to have impaired his
skills. In the doubleheader in Cincinnati he had had
five hits, including his 33rd home run. On his first
day back after the funeral, facing Warren Spahn, he
hit No. 34 off Spahn, but that wasn't news. In the
fourth inning, he reached first base with two out and
Henry Thompson lined a single to right. Mays raced
to third, the throw coming in to second baseman
Danny O'Connell. When O'Connell kept faking
throws at Mays, to drive him back to the bag, Mays
suddenly lit out for the plate and scored as O'Connell
threw high.

Yet the Giants lost. My conclusion is that Mays' bat
was there, along with his speed and daring, but his
spirit was crimped by his aunt's death. A few days
later Mays hit 35 and 36 (the longest home runs he
would hit that year), and Durocher moved Mays into
the number 4 spot. Willie began to spray his line
shots, and the Giants resumed their winning ways.

Mays' performance during the tailspin is one answer to a curiously stubborn indictment that he does
not hit in the clutch. Here was a man carrying a team
singlehandedly until the slump ended, and then when
the team got hot, he put on his 21-game hitting
string.

Just as in 1951, there were great days for Mays,

except many more of them. In August, after another team slump in which the Giants lost three in a row to the Dodgers, Mays exploded for a four-for-four day against Philadelphia, including a triple and a stolen base, and the losing streak ended. In a three-game set at Ebbets Field in early July, Mays was the chief executioner in a 5-2, 10-2, and 11-2 sweep, hitting his 27th home run in the first game, his 28th in the second, and his 29th and 30th in the third. It was Mays' 14th-inning home run that enabled Sal Maglie to beat the Cubs in a game at the end of April. On May 24 Mays had two home runs and four RBI's in a 5-4 win over the Phils. On June 3 in St. Louis, when the Giants beat the Cards, 13-8, Mays and Henry Thompson were the whole show: Mays' two home runs drove in five runs, and Thompson's three home runs drove in the other eight! It was the greatest day in the career of the tragic Hank Thompson, who was washed up in big-league ball less than three years later because he could not handle his whisky, and who finally held up a liquor store in Houston and wound up in a Texas jail with a ten-year sentence. Paroled finally, Thompson died in Fresno, Calif. of a heart attack in 1969.

In a game that same stirring season, Bill Taylor hit a pinch-hit home run in the tenth inning to shade the Braves, 1-0, but it was a throw by Mays in the seventh inning that kept the game alive. Henry Aaron was out at the plate, trying to score on a long fly by Bill Bruton to centerfield. You know how fast Aaron is.

Five times in a row Mays hit home runs in his first

trip to the plate; these home runs in consecutive games tied a club record. The next year he hit home runs in six straight games.

If it wasn't one talent, it was another. On August 29, with two out in St. Louis, bottom of the ninth, score tied, and Joe Cunningham on first, Solly Hemus doubled on the hit-and-run. Mays pursued the ball into right-centerfield and made one of his great throws (some say he had never made a better one) to nail Cunningham at the plate and keep the game going. This time the fever didn't stick. The Cards won in the 11th, 5-4. When the Giants started their final western trip, Mays led them to a 5-1 win in Chicago—the team's seventh straight—with two triples and a double. Even on days that went sour, there was magic enough. In Pittsburgh one day, Mays was twice picked off base, yet his single drove in the winning run in a 2-1 contest. And in the game at Ebbets Field that clinched the pennant, with Sal Maglie tormenting the Dodgers, 7-1, Mays chipped in with three hits.

By this time, thanks to Jane Douglass, Dick Kleiner, and the Tula Music Company, fans were singing, *Say Hey, The Willie Mays Song.* If you don't remember, these were the lyrics:

> *He covers center like he had jet shoes,*
> *The other batters get the Willie blues.*
> *Anything hit his way is out,*
> *It just don't pay them boys to clout!*

> *When Willie served his Uncle Sam,*
> *He let the Giants in an awful jam;*

WILLIE MAYS

But now he's back, he's Leo's joy,
And Willie's still a growing boy.

There was a *Say Hey* chorus in there somewhere,
and if you didn't know the words, you just had to sit
in the Polo Grounds that summer and hear them
blared through the public-address system. If you pre-
ferred, there was another Willie Mays song that year,
Amazin' Willie Mays.

Then the World Series.

In 1954 the Cleveland Indians had won 111 games
on their way to the American League pennant. No
American League team had ever won more: the Yankees, considered by many the best team ever to play
baseball, won 110. In the National League Frank
Chance's Chicago Cubs had won 116 back in 1906,
inspired, no doubt, by the famous ol' double-play trio
of Tinker-to-Evers-to-Chance, but other than that, no
team had ever won as many games in a single season
as the 1954 Indians.

It was a pretty good club, but it never impressed
this old and prejudiced hand. Its front-line pitching
was superb—Bob Lemon, Early Wynn and Mike Gar-
cia, but its bullpen strength was slightly less than that
of the Giants. It had power with Larry Doby and Al
Rosen, but its sixth, seventh, eighth, and ninth spots
were close to automatic outs. Its defense was vulner-
able and it had little speed. While waiting on line at
the bleacher entrance the day the Series opened, I
remember hearing a young Puerto Rican saying ex-
citedly and in contempt, "Indians couldn't even beat
Cardinals." St. Louis finished sixth that year, and it
may have been a National League impertinence to

114

suggest that a sixth-place team would have beaten the team that had won more games in its league than any American League team had ever won, but I am not so sure. The Cards might have beaten the Cleveland we saw those four days at the end of September, start of October.

The Indians, favored by 8-5 to win the Series and favored after each loss to win the next day's game, didn't win a game. The Indians scored six earned runs in the four-game series. Dusty Rhodes drove in seven runs. It was the worst World Series beating one team had given another since the Yankees had beaten Cincinnati four straight back in 1939. (I am not overlooking the Yankees' four-straight over the Phils in 1950; three of those contests were one-run affairs, 1-0, 2-1, and 3-2, and the fourth game, 5-2; I believe the Yankee superiority over the 1950 Phils was not as great as everyone has since assumed.)

But it is not the '54 Series that particularly concerns me. My story is Mays. In the four games, Mays hit .286, with three singles and a double in 14 at-bats, plus four walks. He drove in two runs, scored four, and stole a base. He also made a catch.

It was this catch that is the most remembered incident of that whole Series, of the whole sporting year. You may remember Dusty Rhodes, his slow arrogant walk from the dugout, his red face and his upper-cutting swing; you may remember Rhodes, the individual, better than Mays that 1954 Series, but you remember The Catch more acutely than any other moment.

It was the top of the eighth inning in a bitterly,

painfully slowly played ball game, score 2-2, none out. A base hit by Al Rosen off Al Dark's bare right hand had just driven Sal Maglie to the dressing-room and sent Larry Doby to second. Don Liddle was the pitcher, brought in to throw left-handed curves to left-handed hitting Vic Wertz who, everybody knew, couldn't hit curves served by a left-hander.

So Liddle threw up a swift curve at the shoulders, ready to sweep the center of the plate—practically a crime against nature, as pitching law goes. You throw your fast balls high and tight and your curves low and away; Liddle had violated the code, and now he paid. Wertz hit this curve on a high screaming line to dead centerfield.

I was sitting halfway up the left-centerfield bleachers, where my inverted snobbism used to invite me to sit, and I am not exaggerating when I say no baseball writer in the world had a better view of what next transpired. I watched Mays turn full around, head down, running as hard as he could straight toward the runway between the two bleacher sections, running toward me, as the ball overhead raced him for the wall.

I do not pretend that his catch was the greatest I had ever seen. Mays later said, earnestly and without any thought of whether he was being modest or not, "I thought I had it all the way."

I thought so too, albeit with flickers of doubt. A great catch must be the one that you do not suspect can be made. I had seen Fred Lindstrom, when he briefly played outfield for the Giants because lame legs no longer permitted him to play an adequate third base, run to the bullpen and beyond it in right-centerfield for a gigantic high fly ball struck by the Pirates' Gus Suhr. Lindstrom ran as far as he could and then, still on the dead run, leaped as high as he could leap and snared the ball with a one-handed gloved stab, his body crashing full against the fence. Lindstrom went down in a heap on his back, his gloved hand lying palm up in his lap and the speck of white still showing. After a spell he got up, quite groggy, still holding the ball. You cannot make a better catch than that, unless you leave your glove home.

But Lindstrom had slowed down that year and I believe Mays would have been standing at the wall, ready to jump and catch the ball Lindstrom had grabbed on the run. I believe that Lindstrom could not have reached the ball Wertz hit.

Mays never left his feet for Wertz's drive. All he did was outrun the ball. It was enough. I don't think any centerfielder I have ever seen—neither the Di-Maggio brothers, nor Terry Moore, Eddie Roush, Earle Combs, nor Duke Snider—could have done it, because nobody I have ever seen was as fast in breaking for a ball hit directly over his head. Perhaps Paul Blair, today, is as fast.

And so Mays raced, head down, risking one tiny glance over his left shoulder as he ran, to make sure he had calculated correctly. As he drew close to the large rectangular green screen in front of the right-centerfield section of the bleachers—now I saw him at a slight angle, a three-quarters view of his left front most prominent, 50 or 60 feet away, as compared to over 500 feet away from the press box behind home plate—Mays slowed a trifle to keep from running into the wall. He put his hands head high in front of his left shoulder like a large cup and caught the ball, a football end catching a leading pass in the end zone.

I am iconoclastic enough to think that the throw that followed outshone the catch. Mays agrees. Runners on first and second, remember, and Willie making a catch running away, his back to the diamond, nearly 450 feet from home plate. Yet he was able to whirl in front of the screen, head twisting to his left as his right arm swept around, the inevitable cap falling off, and a baseball gunned to Dave Williams, standing at second base. Doby took third; the badly shaken Rosen retreated in ashen awe back to first. Mays had broken the back of the Indian attack.

You will say I am exaggerating when I add that a throw two innings later strikes me as a better all-around play than the catch on Wertz in the eighth. If the catch on Wertz truly broke the back of the Indian attack, the play in the tenth broke their hearts.

With none out in the tenth, Wertz got his fourth hit of the day, a long blast into the open alley of left-centerfield, directly between Irvin and Mays. Willie raced for the ball as it bounded swiftly toward the junction of the left-centerfield stands and the bleachers. If the ball had got through and reached the wall, it undoubtedly would have been a three-base hit for Wertz.

Coming from his post in centerfield, Mays was aimed at the left-field bullpen at the Polo Grounds; he waved Irvin off with his left hand so that they would not run into each other. Then, 30 feet short of the juncture of stands and bleachers—short of the wall—Willie scooped up the ball on the dead run with his bare hand and, twisting his body on the run, fired the ball to third. Wertz was held to a mighty double.

A man on second base, nobody out, is bad enough, but a man on third is usually disastrous. Mays shut off that disaster, and Rudy Regalado, running for Wertz, didn't score.

Then in the Giant half of the tenth the Indians made a defensive gesture that may have cost them the game. They inserted Mickey Grasso behind the plate. When Grasso appeared in catching regalia, I searched my scorecard for his name; it wasn't listed. There is some fine irony here. Mickey Grasso had broken a leg earlier that year and did not rejoin the Indians until sometime after September 1. To be eligible for World Series participation, a player must be on a team's roster by September 1. But the Indians, sorely beset with injuries and carrying, in addition to their veteran catcher, Jim Hegan, only an untried rookie, Hal Naragon, asked for a waiver of the September 1 deadline in Grasso's case. The dispensation was granted. Grasso took his place behind the plate as the Giant tenth inning opened.

With one out, Willie Mays walked for the second time that day. The first time he had walked, the Giants scored two runs. And on the first pitch to the next batter, Henry Thompson, Mays broke for second. The strategy was obvious. If Mays successfully stole second, the Indians would intentionally walk left-handed-hitting Hank Thompson, whose single had earlier driven in the tying run, in order that Lemon might then pitch to right-handed Monte Irvin. Then, as everybody could have guessed, Durocher would ditch Irvin and send Dusty Rhodes in to hit.

Mays is now a far more accomplished and clever base-stealer than he was back in 1954, although he is perhaps a hair slower. On this occasion, with Lemon pitching and Grasso catching, Mays did not get a good break, but Grasso, leaping out of his squat from behind the plate, threw poorly. The ball bounced in the dirt, about 15 feet in front of second base, and as shortstop Sam Dente waited helplessly for the ball to come down and sink into his glove, Mays—bad start and all—easily slid into second. Dente did not attempt a tag.

And so the next day's box-score had Mays going hitless. Yet without his two walks and stolen base, it is likely that the Giants would not have won the ball game. Without The Catch, they couldn't have won.

For win it—and quickly—they did. Thompson was walked. Rhodes batted for Irvin. Lemon, worn down by the terrible pressure of keeping his curve ball low and away for more than nine innings so that no Giant could pull it toward the inviting foul poles, let a curve slip. It came in half-speed and chest-high, and Dusty slapped it softly into the first row of seats near the right-field foul line, the ball nudged gently along by a fresh breeze, for a three-run home run. Mays trotted the bases at a slow, near-imperious pace, pointing to each as he touched it to remind Thompson and Rhodes behind him to make sure they, too, touched them all. The Giants had won, 5-2.

Willie Mays, late that coming winter, signed a contract for the 1955 season that called for his being paid $40,000. Nobody took a gun and shot him. As a matter of fact, all during 1954 Horace Stoneham, the man who would have done the gun-shooting, slipped Mays $1,000 here and $1,000 there, under the counter. By the time the season had ended, Mays was earning $25,000 for his work in 1954. None of this includes any of the television-commercial and other gravy monies—between $10,000 and $15,000—or the $11,147.90 he received as his winner's share of the World Series loot.

There could be no doubt about it. Willie Mays had become the highest-paid stickball player in the whole world.

Chapter Nine

During the wonderful doings of 1954, a congressional investigating committee turned its attention to the pampering of athletes in the armed forces. On May 5, 1954—the day before Willie Mays became 23 years old—it was charged that he had been coddled by the Army. Willie was not the only athlete involved, but he was the most prominent. The committee insisted that he had to be absolved of any role in what it termed the "shenanigans" of the case. Willie had not asked nor sought in any way to be assigned to 20-plus months of ballplaying. He was the pawn. Whether the committee then delved into the question of who was to blame—what Army higher-up or individual had sought preferential treatment for Mays—is not known here. The story died quietly.

But with the story, and with the previous fuss over Mays' having flunked his AGCT, just a tiny bit of the gloss was rubbed off. Willie lost his halo. After the 1954 Series had ended, Willie received so many awards, trophies, and plaques he could have opened a hardware store. He beat out Ted Kluszewski for the season's Most Valuable Player award, the first player to win in his first full year. It wasn't a complete runaway only because a few writers close to the Giants scattered their votes between John Antonelli and Alvin Dark. One writer openly admitted voting for Dark not because he thought the Giant shortstop and captain was the most valuable—"Hell," he said, "Mays is more valuable than an unlimited expense account"—but because Dark was then over 30 years old and the writer sensed rightly that Dark would never have as good a year in the future, whereas Mays would have many more shots at the honor. (With all those shots at the MVP award, Mays did not win a second time until eleven years later, in 1965.) Even with this kind of tortured thinking, Willie won easily and won everything else.

To keep him away from most of the winter banquet circuit (it has never done anything to a player except make him fat and acquaint him with a baseball martini—four parts gin, one part cigar smoke), the Giants shipped their most precious employee to Santurce, Puerto Rico, to perform in a winter league.

For a spell Willie was more popular in Puerto Rico than Governor Luiz Munoz Marin, or even rum. Fans in Santurce, a city just below San Juan, learned to chant *Ole! Mira!* (Say Hey) whenever Willie came up, and in response Mays would blast another dent in the fences of Parque Sixto Escobar.

The Santurce team, which ran away with the pennant, was managed by Herman Franks. It included, besides Mays, Ruben Gomez, the Pirates' Bob Clemente, and a host of old friends from Mays' Negro League days. A fat, blubbery youngster named Orlando Cepeda rode the bench. The ubiquitous Frank Forbes was along too, so Mays was not lonely, and Santurce owner Pedro Zorilla liked to thrust a pig onto a spit and treat his ballplayers to this great delicacy over at his beach house at Mar Chiquita.

A pleasant way to spend the winter. Except that it may have been just too much baseball for Mays. Not that it could be detected in his play. He began by hitting over .400, "slacked" off to lead the league with .395, and was voted, naturally, the league's Most Valuable Player.

But before the award, Willie ran into trouble. On January 11, 1955, Bob Clemente, taking his practice swings, decided to change bats. As Clemente stepped out, Ruben Gomez, a pitcher who always enjoyed hitting, quickly leaped into the cage and told batting-practice pitcher Milton Ralat to throw to him until Clemente returned.

This might have been okay, except that Gomez was jumping the gun. After Clemente Mays was the next scheduled hitter. Ralat refused to pitch to Gomez, and—according to one of several versions—Gomez sat down in a sulk on home plate. Mays stepped to a corner of the cage and directed Ralat to throw to him. Ralat threw and Mays drilled a hot shot back at the pitcher, striking him on the shoulder. Ralat is said to have called Mays a name, and as the pitcher and Mays moved toward each other in anger, Gomez jumped up, still holding his bat. Gomez says that he merely wanted to get in between the two players and pry them apart (with a bat?), but when Willie saw Gomez coming at him, he closed in on Ruben instead. In the ensuing skirmish, Mays is credited with landing a short straight right-hand punch that dropped Gomez. The rest of the tale has manager

Herman Franks pulling Mays off and Mays allegedly saying to Franks, "Are you on the Puerto Ricans' side, too?"

When Mays made his next appearance, San Juan fans booed him loudly. Willie promptly slugged a triple, to beat San Juan 3-2. A few days later, claiming a knee injury, he returned to the Sates. Back home, both Mays and Gomez minimized the incident and Franks practically insisted that it never took place at all. There was never afterward any visible sign of antagonism between Mays and Gomez, nor anything to indicate that Mays carries any ill-feeling for any of the players who have come up from the Caribbean to join the Giants in recent years.

But echoes remain, some of them nasty. In the dreary year of 1960, rumors had the Giants divided into three parts: the Stateside Negroes, led by Willie Mays; the Latin Americans, led by Orlando Cepeda; and the Stateside white players (a poor trampled minority, no doubt) .

Now everything was wrong with the Giants in 1960, and in a year like that, any reason for disaster must be credited. The Giants undoubtedly had their cliques. Whether they were formed along racial or national lines has never been confirmed and never can be. In the summer of 1964 manager Alvin Dark was said to have cast aspersion on the mentality and alertness of his Negro and Latin ballplayers, but Willie Mays, Monte Irvin, and Hank Thompson have all stated over and over that they never noted any sign of prejudice in the Southern-born Dark. In any event, it is foolish to charge Willie Mays with leading one dissident group against another.

For one thing, Mays is something of a loner. He is not psychologically constituted to whip together a faction for any reason except, perhaps, to repair on the nearest pool hall. As for Willie's not getting on with the Latin American Giants, there is evidence to the contrary. In 1958 it was Mays who took Felipe Alou in hand (so Alou himself says) and helped him get used to big-league parks. Mays even let Alou run over from rightfield to grab fly balls away from Mays in dead centerfield—an outfielding felony. Before he was traded to the Braves, Alou used to say, "People refer to the Giants as 'Willie Mays and Company.' Well, I am proud to be part of that company." When his younger brother, Matty, joined the Giants, Felipe took him aside and said, "If you need help, you go to Willie." And when the youngest brother Jesus came along, Felipe and Matty said, "You need help, see Willie."

In an early 1961 training session at Arizona, I saw Mays and Juan Marichal engage in friendly horseplay, Mays tripping Marichal on the sly and always in obvious pleasantry.

Those who would find such factionalism chortled in glee after the Marichal-Roseboro incident of August 22, 1965. A New York newspaper columnist said the fracas indicated that Negro players and Latin American players did not like each other "one little bit." Writers were quick to point out that Mays went to the side of Roseboro, a Dodger, rather than to Marichal, a Giant.

WILLIE MAYS

Willie Mays is a human being; he went to a friend's side. Roseboro is a close friend of Mays, and it was Roseboro, not Marichal, whose face streamed blood. Had it been Marichal who was battered, Mays would have rushed to his teammate's aid and helped *him* to the dressing room.

Still, the Puerto Rico incident occurred in some form or other, and Willie Mays did engage in fisti-cuffs with Ruben Gomez, a Latin ballplayer. What does it prove? Nothing at all, except that players would rather take batting practice than eat, that Willie Mays was younger than he is today, and that for all his bubbling warmth he is not unlike the rest of us snappish, petulant mortals. And anyway, it was pretty hot that day in Puerto Rico.

That the outside world of Puerto Rico and humid weather and petulance impinged on Willie Mays probably comes as a surprise to many of us. We like to place our baseball heroes in a showcase, untouched by anything other than the breeze set off by a Koos-man pitch. The world is too much with some and not enough with others, but even with wide-eyed children it's there. If the world did not affect Willie Mays, he probably would hit .600, sandwiched between stick-ball games, and people would yawn at his name.

But Mays hits .300 and people cheer. Some of them boo.

In February, 1956, Dennis Holt, a white student at the University of Alabama, received a letter from Willie Mays. The University of Alabama was at that moment the scene of ugly riots resulting from a court decision that a Negro girl, Authurine Lucy, be admitted to previously all-white classes. Miss Lucy was barred from school, allegedly because of the physical dangers involved. Young Holt took a courageous stand against the rioters within his own race, and Mays threw his weight behind the youngster. The ballplayer wrote, in part:

"It is incumbent for you younger generation of white boys and girls to repudiate this action."

Unfortunately, neither Holt's stand nor Mays' influence counted enough, and other white students were either unable or unwilling to generate support. Miss Lucy was forced to quit Alabama U. It is not my purpose to laud Mays for his action, just as it was not my aim to criticize Mays for the fist fight in Puerto Rico. I cite the letter to Holt merely to show that Mays' world obviously extends beyond the foul lines of a baseball diamond.

That it is indeed broader than we had supposed became startlingly evident the very day after Dennis Holt received Mays' letter.

On February 14, 1956, St. Valentine's Day, Willie Mays got married. He and his bride-to-be, Marghuerite Wendelle Kenny Chapman, sped off to Elkton, Maryland, the Atlantic seaboard's answer to the marriage mills of Nevada. And "sped" is the right word. Willie and his year-old green Cadillac were stopped for speeding on the Jersey Turnpike, and Mays paid a fine of $15 before proceeding to the vows.

Mays' marriage came as a total shock. Ever since his return from the Army, Willie had played the field, and Frank Forbes had been a busy man. During the 1954 season, Forbes one day said to Willie, "Well, boy, you finally made it. You're a real celebrity now. One of the gossip columnists says you're about to get married."

But everybody knew this was just talk (the columnist knew it, too, but she had to fill space); everybody knew Willie was too young to be tied down. It was difficult to imagine this restless mercurial person doing what the rest of us .199 softball hitters do—marry, rear children, walk the dog.

In fact, this is just what Mays did. He and Marghuerite adopted a boy, Michael, early in 1959. Marghuerite's daughter (by one of her two prior marriages) also lived with the Mayses. When *Sports Illustrated* did a lengthy piece on Mays at the outset of the 1959 season, there was a picture of Willie outside his San Francisco home. There was a leash in Mays' hand and at the other end a perky white poodle. On an upstairs balcony, looking like some cool and remote queen, was Marghuerite.

So Willie Mays got married. He said to reporters, "I'm twenty-four years old, and I thought it was about time I settled down."

Marghuerite Mays was a stunning, chic beauty, two years older than Mays. Eyebrows were raised over Willie's union with this sophisticated divorcee. Since that Valentines' Day, rumors hounded the couple.

The rumors had some basis. After one spat in the winter of 1960, Mays stormed out of their New Rochelle home taking his clothes and his portable television set, which just about summed up, and in correct order, his other interests. A few days later he was back (he'd visited his family in Alabama), but not before reporters had got Marghuerite to confirm the brief blowup.

The marriage lasted five years. It came to an official end in a courtroom in San Francisco just before the 1961 All-Star game, with all the usual marital cross-bickering. Mays' lawyer Bergen Van Brunt, said that Marghuerite had spent $400 for shoes and $8,000 for mink. Marghuerite's lawyer, Phillip Adams, said a month later in another courtroom, "It seems that a total of $410,000 has slipped through Mr. Mays' fingers in the past four years."

And that led to the unusual part of the separation proceedings. Willie Mays was flat broke. Edgar P. Feely, treasurer of the San Francisco Giants, said with unconscious cruelty,

"I don't have the exact figures but it looks to me as if Mays doesn't have anything left."

What he had was a $65,000 debt to the Giants for advances against wages they had paid him, plus a debt of $8,641 in back taxes to the federal government.

How did it happen? Even with shoes and minks and a white Cadillac for his wife and a pink Thunderbird for himself and five or six new suits in a single day and maintaining homes in San Francisco and New Rochelle, how did it happen?

No one knows except Mays, and perhaps he doesn't know either. There is no doubt that Mays and Marghuerite lived well. Early in the marriage, when the Mayses lived in upper Manhattan, the house was like a film star's. One wall of the dining room was all mirrors. Over the table hung a heavy chandelier, the crystal like diamonds. The dining table had a wafer-thin glass top and thick, curlicued marble legs. Heavy drapes hung on the wall; a heavy potted plant filled a corner of the room. In the Mays game room were upside-down wine glasses with toothpick-thin stems, baskets of Italian wines, bar stools, and, of course, a velvet-smooth pool table. The bedroom had brocaded drapes, more dripping chandeliers, brocaded bedspreads, and another wall of mirrors.

You cannot say that this affluent style, this pillow-fat elegance, was something totally new which he learned from his wife. Long before he met Marghuerite, Willie wore $250 suits and expensive silk ties with pearl-headed stickpins. So this, too, is a side of Willie Mays.

Not that the outside world helped the couple much. In 1957, when the Giants made it official that they were moving from New York to San Francisco, Mays and Marghuerite began to shop for a home in the city by the Bay. Before you knew it, this man who had brought excitement to millions, and his handsome shapely wife, had become objects of hatred because of their skin color. A $37,500 house in a relatively exclusive section was at first offered to Mays for sale and then withdrawn. George Christopher, then the Mayor of San Francisco and a man who had been instrumental in bringing the Giants out West, jumped in on Mays' side and branded the objectors as bigots. Mays and Marghuerite soon moved in and the story seemed to be over.

It hadn't really begun. On June 20, 1959, the

Braves came to Seals Stadium, and beat the Giants, 4-1, to lead the hysterical National League by one-half game. (Mays drove in the only Giant run.) That night, or rather at 1:30 in the morning, while Mays and his family slept, a soft-drink bottle came crashing through a six-foot by eight-foot front-room window. In the bottle was a piece of paper and on the paper a vile message.

A year-and-a-half had gone by since the Mayses had moved in. During those eighteen months not a single white resident had spoken to Marghuerite Mays. The period was dotted with occasional crank letters and obscene anonymous phone calls. In December, 1959, Willie Mays sold his San Francisco house and moved back to New York.

For a while Mays and Marghuerite lived in New Rochelle. The situation was better, but far from idyllic. Looking back, Mays said, "I didn't even particularly want that San Francisco house in the first place. But once people said we couldn't live there, and the mayor and the rest got involved, then we had to follow through." Far from dramatizing the situation, Mays remarked, "It wasn't as much trouble as the papers said. It didn't bother me too much." With a short, mirthless laugh, he placed the memory in a kind of perspective: "Shoot, man, I know a Negro can't live just anywhere he wants, even in New York, so why figger it's going to be better in San Francisco." He liked it better in New Rochelle, but he did not pretend it was perfect. He said while still living there with Marghuerite, "It's pleasant. The people seem like nice people. I don't know many of them."

And then he added this remarkable description of himself, to explain why he didn't know too many of his neighbors: "I don't pursue people."

It was a dovetailing sentence; so many loose ends slide into place. In spite of all Mays' geniality, there is in this down-to-earth person (and he is down to earth, even with the brocaded drapes and chandeliers) a touch of the aloofness that made DiMaggio so much a loner. Mays is not a complete loner, like DiMaggio, but a bit of one.

His chagrin when the Barons' bus took off without him becames more understandable. He was not used to pursuing people then either. On the road with the Giants, Mays rooms alone now. He used to share a room with Irvin and later with Bill White and briefly with André Rodgers, but now he prefers to be alone. It is not because he is a great star with star's prerogatives. He does not pursue people.

Back in 1956, when Mays got married, he submitted to an interview, meeting newsmen while clad in his pale-ivory pajamas, answering their questions in bed. He declared, with a scarcely inaudible sniff, that people said he was going to marry this girl or that, but—he touched his heart—"I'm the only one who knows what's in here."

Chapter Ten

The years 1955, 1956, and 1957 form a plateau between the great deeds of 1954 and the present-day San
Francisco performer. It is a bumpy plateau, reflecting
the jitters of a briefly fine club quickly falling apart.
In 1955, the year the Yankees didn't win the World
Series, the Giants finished third. In 1956 Leo Durocher was through, Bill Rigney was the new manager,
and the Giants were sixth. In 1957 they were sixth
again.

Not only was it an inferior, aging team; it had quit
on itself. In the Giant locker room after losses in '56
or '57, the ballplayers dressed in silence or sat, heads
down, eyes absently fixed on a question-mark future
or a happier past. Men walked aimlessly about, bare-
foot, or sat reading their scant fanmail, or hurried to
get out of the dank sepulchral clubhouse. The team
would wake up when John Antonelli threw his annual champagne treat in the clubhouse near the end of
the season but even then the loudest noise was a cork
popping, the most animation the bubbles in a glass.
Mays didn't touch the stuff; twice was enough. Manager Rigney did not have the natural ebullience of
Durocher; he was a silent man, tortured by what was
happening, his gray hair turning white—a wrinkled

cadaver of a man who was not yet forty years old but sometimes looked nearer sixty.

In 1955 Mays laid to rest two myths: that his very presence insured a pennant and that he couldn't play on a team that didn't win. He hit .319, second best in the league, and among his 185 hits were 51 home runs. No Giant—except Mays himself in 1965—has ever hit more. His 13 triples tied him with Dale Long for the league lead. He drove in 127 runs, his career peak until he topped the figure in 1962 with a whopping 141 RBI's. He led the league for the second year in a row in slugging percentage. His total bases, 382, remain a personal high, equalled in 1962. It was the first year that Mays began to steal bases in clusters, 24 steals in 28 attempts.

It was also the year he hit seven home runs in six consecutive games and the year he practically tore down Ebbets Field with his bat: nine home runs against the Dodgers in 11 games at Brooklyn. Mays hit 29 of his home runs on the road, and 22 at home. So much for the Polo Grounds and the cheap fences.

In the All-Star game in Milwaukee, Willie ran along the wire fence into right-centerfield, then leaped up, his glove a foot and a half above the top rung of the wire, to rob Ted Williams of a home run. At bat, his single off Whitey Ford started a two-run rally in the seventh; his second single, with two out in the eighth, sparked a three-run rally. The National League won, 6-5.

Yet in 1955 they booed Willie Mays.

It began in a ball game in August at the Polo Grounds, with a man on second and two out. Duke

Snider hit a sinking line drive to centerfield, and Mays rushed in, hoping to make a shoestring grab and close the inning, or else short-hop the ball and have a play on the runner coming home. Mays missed connections altogether, the ball skipping under his glove and rolling to the runway in centerfield. When the ball finally came to rest, it was 500 feet from home plate. Mays took one backward look at the ball and refused to waste himself running after it. The runner from second and Snider both scored.

The crowd, shocked at what it considered an obvious failure to hustle, let loose its jeers, no doubt instigated by the Dodger fans aching for retaliation for the mayhem Mays had committed across the river.

Newsman Joe King wrote a piece for publication the next day, reeking with hyperbole, but still probably touching a truth:

"Maybe success did come too fast for the young man. Maybe the dramatic Negro boy the Giants plucked out of deep South obscurity has failed to appreciate that last year [1954] was a freak and that baseball is a job you work at 60 minutes an hour, and that the prima donnas are hated worse than any other by the fans. That's what Willie was yesterday—a prima donna."

Of course, the Giants hadn't rescued Mays from deep South obscurity; if they hadn't signed him, the Braves or White Sox or somebody would have, and you might say that Mays plucked the *Giants* from second-division obscurity. Nor was 1954 a freak. Still, there was the uncontested fact that Mays did not chase the ball. He must have known that base runners occasionally fall down on the basepaths; sometimes they miss a bag and have to retreat to make contact. Runners pull up lame. There wasn't much chance that Mays could have thrown out a-one-legged man or Ernie Lombardi from the spot where the ball finally died, had he chosen to race back after muffing the shoestring try, but that is never the question. You run and throw anyway.

So the fans booed and made life noisy for a week or two—the most fun the Polo Grounds had heard all year—and Mays proved that the signal of maturity is cynicism when he said, "They'll cheer me when I get a hit." He went on an astonishing home-run binge, and the crowd loved him in September as they had in May.

Yet the memory lingers on. In San Francisco Willie has been booed pretty heavily at times, but then the fans had been told to expect a superman and they got only the best player in the world. They booed him very loudly in the game of May 8, 1959, when all he did was hit a single, a triple and a double in his first three times up, steal two bases, and score from third base on a soft fly ball to second-baseman Charley Neal. But in the eighth inning, the Giants losing 2-1 despite these heroics, Mays came up again, with Jim Davenport on third, and Felipe Alou on second, one man out. Dodger pitcher Stan Williams decided to walk Mays, but with the count 3-and-0, Mays swung at the fourth pitch, even though it was far outside. He popped out, the rally died, the Giants lost, and the fans let Mays have it. Mays said after the game, "It was a bad play. I was trying too hard to win." This more or less sums up the incident.

In a game in St. Louis in 1956, the year after the booing at the Polo Grounds, Mays lifted a fly ball behind the plate. He stood in the batter's box. A light breeze wafted the ball into fair territory, where the Cardinal catcher grabbed it for the out. Mays was fined $25 by Manager Bill Rigney for not running. The fine was rescinded almost immediately and Rigney announced loudly that Mays was "the hustlingest player I've ever seen."

And on April 22, 1960, at Wrigley Field, in a game the Giants won 10-8, Mays hit a fly ball to left field in the sixth inning and didn't run hard. The wind carried the ball over the head of Frank Thomas, and Mays got only a double on a ball that should have gone for three bases. Mays criticized himself after the game (just as it had been he who said after not running out the foul-fair ball in St. Louis, "I ought to be fined for that"), but within the criticism is some faint self-justification:

"I don't run myself crazy, tire myself, on balls I think are easy outs. I like to have something in reserve when it counts. I guess I got to watch myself a little closer. That was a bad play, and I know it."

The ball on Snider in 1955, the pop at the plate in 1956, and the double that should have been a triple four years later are the three recorded instances of Willie Mays' not going all out on a ball field. Perhaps there have been a few others. But even if there have been, the lapses are so rare that they add to the feeling that few players around try harder than does Mays.

In 1956, after Mays' 51-home-run season and the league's second best batting average, he tumbled to his first full year under .300—.296, to be exact—and even worse, a runs-batted-in total of 84, a comedown of 40 runs from the year before. Yet in this "ghastly" year, Willie Mays became the first ballplayer in history to hit more than 30 home runs and steal more than 30 bases in a single season. He had 36 home runs; he stole 40 bases, the first of four consecutive years he was to lead the league. In the words of Ty Cobb, Mays restored the art of stealing third base. In 13 attempts, he stole third base 13 times.

Nobody voted Mays to the All-Star team in 1956, but manager Walt Alston added him to the squad, so Mays hit a pinch-hit home run of some 400 feet off Whitey Ford. Indeed, Willie has had a bit of luck against Ford; in seven trips in exhibitions and All-Star games Mays got seven hits off Ford. That is, up until the 1962 World Series, when the two men met in something more important than exhibition gallivanting. In the Series opener Mays promptly got three more hits in a row off Ford before Whitey finally got him out.

The year 1956 was the Giants' first under Rigney, and though Mays insisted then that he had no trouble playing for Rig, it wasn't true. Willie has trouble adjusting to nearly anything new. In 1960, when Rigney was fired and Tom Sheehan took over, Mays said he'd have to get used to playing for Sheehan *just as he had to get used to playing for Rigney* when Durocher left. And 1956 was also the first year of Mays' marriage.

In 1957, before increasing empty stands, Mays was once again a hitting machine. In 1954 the Giants had played for over 1,500,000 fans at home. Now the attendance barely exceeded 650,000. Yet in this dispiriting atmosphere Mays hit .333, again second in the league, and for the third time in four seasons he led the league in slugging. Also for the third time in four seasons he led in three-base hits, with a staggering 20. No other active ballplayer today has ever hit so many triples in one big-league season. Mays became the first player in the league's history to hit 20 or more doubles, triples, and home runs in the same year. He led both leagues in stolen bases. For the second time in a row, and the third time since Abner Doubleday didn't invent baseball, Mays hit 30 or more home runs (35) and stole 30 or more bases (38). You went to the Polo Grounds that year—all 653,923 of you—not to see the Giants, but to see Mays. He was the complete ballplayer.

Bothered by a bad leg, he limped into the 1957 All-Star game and hit a triple off Billy Pierce and a single off Early Wynn. Unbothered in April, he beat out an infield hit in a game against the Phils, took second when the ball was thrown away, stole third, and scored the winning run on a short single. A month later, at Wrigley Field, he went from first to third on a ground out and then stole home. All year long he was travelling from first to third on ground-balls outs or on infield hits. A couple times he scored from second on ground outs. Infielders started to hurry their throws when Mays ran the bases, and opposing teams began to make errors; this was Mays' value to the Giants—impossible to measure. For years Jackie Robinson had been the finest runner in the game. Not the fastest; just the smartest, the most daring. Now Willie Mays was the best. Again, not the fastest. Bill Bruton would have beaten Mays by a full stride or two in a 100-yard dash. But Bruton just wasn't Mays on the bases. Willie had learned, to the nearest hair, just how long a lead he could get away with; he studied every catcher in the league, every pitcher's move. He knew that Wilmer Mizell would always throw fast balls with Mays on base, so that the ball would get up to the plate faster, but Mizell apparently didn't know that Mays had spotted a flaw in the pitcher's equipment. When Mizell did throw his fast ball, he kicked his right leg higher and thus took a trifle longer to release the ball. So Mays ran wild on Mizell, and it wasn't until 1960 that the pitcher figured out what was wrong. This is ballplaying: a great talent refined by craft to a point of art.

Unfortunately, nobody seemed to notice. The crowds thinned each day; the noise lessened. Finally Horace Stoneham announced at a press conference on August 19, 1957: "We're going to San Francisco in 1958."

Somebody asked Stoneham: "How do you feel about the kids in New York from whom you are taking the Giants?"

"I feel bad about the kids," Stoneham answered. "I've seen lots of them at the Polo Grounds. But I haven't seen many of their fathers lately."

The season drew to an end, and I flew from California to New York to watch the Giants play the last two games they would ever play in New York. I wandered about the Polo Grounds that last weekend in September, 1957, talking to ushers, ice-cream vendors, men's room attendants and fans, and I sat in the bleachers next to Louis Kleppel, the man who used to collect money from other fans so that he could buy watches for Giant ballplayers. Kleppel travelled with the Giants in 1951, and every day before the game he would shake hands with Bobby Thomson—give Thomson what Kleppel called a "psychokinetic push." (So maybe it wasn't Mays' presence in '51, but Kleppel's.)

And we watched Willie Mays. There was a sign in left field that read, "Go, Team, Go," and they did not mean it the way the hippies do; they meant it literally. Get out. But there was another sign: "Stay, Willie, Stay." Let San Francisco have the Giants; New York would keep Mays.

Mays performed his artistic prodigies that last day. Hardly noticeable ones. In an early inning a Pirate drilled a ball into left-centerfield, between Rhodes and Mays, which rolled all the way to the wall beyond the bullpen. Mays stationed himself in medium-deep left centerfield. Rhodes hustled after the ball and threw it to Mays. Then Mays turned and threw on one bounce to the plate a tremendous throw, just to remind New York what throwing was like, and the Pirate runner was out trying to stretch his triple. But the true beauty of the play was the way Mays handled Rhodes' throw. Rhodes had never boasted of his ability in the field (he used to say, "I can't field and I've got a lousy arm, but I sure love to whack at that ball,"), and in this instance his relay to Mays was one of those tricky short hops, landing two feet in front of Mays. Somehow Mays managed to trap the ball, his back to the diamond; then he whirled and threw. Another man would have been lucky just to have come up cleanly with Rhodes' throw.

That was one silent moment. In the stands they had roared when the Giant catcher put the tag on the man for the out, but nobody had noticed the legerdemain that made the play possible.

There was a more startling moment, and this one did elicit cheers. Mays hit a ground ball to third—a perfectly ordinary ground ball, not a topped roller or a tricky Baltimore chop, but just a ground ball, the kind you see hit in fielding practice and a dozen times during every game. The Pirate third baseman came up cleanly with the ball and nonchalantly made his routine play, a lob toss to first base. Not a bad throw; just a perfectly ordinary throw. Mays beat it out for an infield hit. He had actually stolen a base hit, running on that last day as though a pennant were at stake (the Giants lost, 9-1). This was the man they'd once booed for failing to chase a ball that had slipped through him to the bleacher runway. It was the first time I had ever seen a man beat out a routine ground ball that had been fielded cleanly.

Then in the ninth inning of that last day, a gray Sunday, Mays came to bat for the last time as a New York Giant. There was a sizable round of applause as he took his last stance. He shifted his feet around, his head down. A pitch came in and another, and the count was one-and-one, and all the time the applause kept building, over 11,000 fans rising out of their seats. Pretty soon the applause was so loud that Mays had to acknowledge it. He stepped out of the box and touched his hand to his cap. It was, to me, another first.

I do not recall hearing another ovation given a man after the pitcher has started to work on him. The whole business was unsettling to Mays. "I never felt so nervous," he has since said. "My hands were shaking. It was worse than any World Series game. I tried to hit a home run. I tried very hard to show them how I felt. I wanted to do something for the fans."

He tried too hard, the way a man will, and hit a ground ball to short. He was out at first, and when he trotted back to the Giant dugout, the applause followed him. Dusty Rhodes hit another ground ball to short; the Giants had lost their fourth ball game in a row, and the Giant tenancy at the Polo Grounds was over. The fans poured onto the field, running right past and over the stadium guards. They tore up the bases and uprooted home plate, ripped the fences and the bullpen benches, and chased the players all the way to the dressing-room stairs. Mays ran to the clubhouse, his cap to his breast: "I was scared. I thought they were going to tear me apart." If they had, it would have been an act of love.

Chapter Eleven

Willie Mays does not pretend to be Gentleman Bobby Richardson or Little Lord Fauntleroy. But like Richardson and like gentlemanly Gil Hodges before, Mays has never been thrown out of a baseball game. At the plate, except for a slightly raised left eyebrow or a brief turn of the head, eyes widened in almost pained disbelief, Mays never dresses down an umpire on a called pitch. Although he has been involved in an unlimited number of close plays at the plate and on the bases, Willie has seldom argued after an umpire has decided one against him. Once, a few years back, Mays kicked up a mild storm after being called out at the plate—by far the noisiest objection he'd lodged against an umpire up till then. Photographs the next day revealed that not only had Mays scored, but that the catcher had not tagged Mays, and even if he had, he did not have the ball. Pictures, like statistics, can lie. Umpires can also be wrong.

In the second play-off game in 1962, Mays tried to advance to third on a base hit, but was called out on a terribly close play. He objected strenuously to the call, and this time photographs make clear only that it had been a terribly close play. The Giants lost the ball game by a single run, and Mays may have been fighting more for the run than for the principle of the thing. This happens to the most honorable ball-players. In another tight contest, this time in 1965, John Roseboro tried to advance to third on a sacrifice bunt, but Jim Davenport made a swift tag and the umpire called Roseboro out. John argued with some vehemence, and later he said, "I *know* I beat the play." The play was on television tape, and when it was re-run, it was plain that Davenport had indeed tagged Roseboro out. Tight ball games and tighter pennant races will do that.

Still, Mays has been in several hundred tight ball games and several tight pennant races, and he has argued so seldom that he appears a mild-mannered, almost obsequious gentleman. He is not. For all his quiet conduct, he is spirited and sometimes more than that. A few infielders and catchers think he is the toughest man on the basepaths today. One of the hardest runners in the game, he hits a base or a baseman with fullback's power. In a game against the Phils in 1965, Mays barreled his 180-plus pounds into a rookie catcher, Pat Corrales, and sent him to a hospital with a mild concussion. Mays himself badly bruised his hip on the play. But what counted—in the game—was that Mays' violence resulted in a run.

This jarring power on the bases has tattooed Mays' body with several dozen bruises; it has also won games. On August 4, 1960, in Philadelphia (it was manager Gene Mauch's contention that Mays played better against the Phils, and in Philadelphia, than he did anywhere else in the league), the Giants spotted the locals a six-run lead in the first two innings. But for once the Giants battled back, and after one of

Willie's three hits had left him on third base with one out, Orlando Cepeda hit a short fly to right field, where Ken Walters, then one of the best-throwing outfielders in the league, caught the ball and threw a strike to the plate. Down the line came Mays, beaten dead by Walters' great throw, until Willie hurled himself, spikes aimed like daggers at rookie catcher Clay Dalrymple. The ball was literally stabbed loose. The Giants went on to score five runs and win the ball game, 8-7.

On April 19, 1961, Mays tried to advance from first after a fly ball to Cincinnati's (then) Frank Robinson. Robinson's throw to Elio Chacon doubled Mays, but Mays' high left foot removed Chacon from the line-up for a couple of weeks. It also caused some resentment. A season or two later Mays found himself again on second base with Chacon the baseman in an attempted pick-off play. Mays ripped into the bag; Chacon fell on top of Mays and began flailing away with his fists. Mays quickly reversed the order of things and simply pinned Chacon to the ground until the players were separated.

That is the way Willie Mays runs bases, and that is the way baseball is played today, the way it has been played all century. I remember with grim amusement the very first game Pee Wee Reese of the Dodgers played in the Polo Grounds. The late Mel Ott—the "nice guy" of Leo Durocher's title song, "Nice Guys Finish Last"—was on first base, and the next Giant hit a ground ball to second. The ball was flipped to Reese, who prepared to make contact with the bag before throwing to first for a double play. Ott hit him. He blasted Reese across the chest and lower ribs, Mel's chunky body parallel to the ground in a flying block that caved in Reese and sent the shortstop one way and the baseball another. It was one of the most flagrant cases of a runner not bothering about the base but dead set on taking out the infielder. It was, you might say, Ott's way of introducing Reese to the nuances of a Giant-Dodger ball game.

In July, 1959, at Seals Stadium, Mays ripped into Chicago catcher Earl Averill on a squeeze play, slicing the catcher's pants to shreds and tearing them so high that it was apparent Mays would have sailed over home plate without making contact had not Averill's body been there to stop the flight. This time Averill did not take kindly to Mays' slide. He and Willie had words, and umpire Ken Burkhart shoved Mays out of the way before the words became sticks and stones. (Mays also hurt his thigh and did not start for two days, he hit a pinch single the next day and a pinch-hit sacrifice fly and a two-run home run the next.)

I doubt that umpire Burkhart was really needed to keep order. Mays never really flips his lid, at least not any more. Gone are the days of Puerto Rico. When an Elio Chacon starts to swing, Mays merely restrains him. But Mays does play hard, and if the new, young, hard-running, swift and spirited Giants of San Francisco were a refreshing change from the 1957 Giants of Thomson and Ray Jablonski, Gail Harris, Ray Katt, Wes Westrum, and Don Mueller, one must also remember that Willie Mays was the key to the '58 team and to all San Francisco Giant teams since.

In 1958, when manager Rigney let loose rookies Jim Davenport, Willie Kirkland, Cepeda, Alou, and catcher Bob Schmidt, none of them played with so white-hot an intensity; none displayed more verve, more desire. Cepeda, on occasion, was a veritable madman, oversliding bases by as much as 25 feet, but he also showed on occasion a dreamy *wanderlust* in the field.

This is the difference between Mays and other red hots in baseball. Willie concentrates his venom on the end result: scoring runs or catching flies or throwing bullets or belting pitched balls. The play is still the thing.

Here is the classic example. In Pittsburgh on May 25, 1958, the Pirates suddenly took toeholds against Ruben Gomez and began whistling line drives all over the park. After Bill Mazeroski peeled off a tremendous foul drive, Gomez reached in for his pet convincer, and Mazeroski threw up his left arm to avoid being skulled. The next inning Vernon Law, a deacon of his church, smacked Gomez with a pitch, and the field swarmed with Pirates, all gathered around Gomez. Manager Danny Murtaugh actually took a few swings at Gomez, who was still holding a bat. Then Orlando Cepeda came bounding out of the Giant dugout, headed for the Pirate mass. And as quickly as that, Willie Mays reached behind Cepeda and with a gorgeous flying tackle nailed Orlando before he could wreak much damage. Cepeda is one of the strongest human beings ever assembled. Mays' tackle let the air out of the balloon.

This is Mays. On a play at second, he will slice an

infielder in quarters, but he hates spilled blood during time out. And those were genuine tears in his eyes when John Roseboro's head split open.

Mays once said, "I've tried to help Cepeda with the umpires and with things like the blow-up in Pittsburgh. I know he gets wild at times and that's not good for him. It's not good to get the umpires against you."

So Willie Mays, the thunder-and-lightning man, the volcano ready to blow, is also a shrewd anchor, weighing down a club that at times tends to drift.

And this is the story of the big move westward. San Francisco fans, expecting not only Superman but also the bubbling Say Hey kid of legend, the spirit that not only walks, but hops, skips, and jumps on water, were somewhat disappointed. The rap is not at Mays, but at San Francisco.

In 1958, the first year there, Mays hit .347, his highest mark to date. He led the league in base hits that season, with 208; he's never made more. He failed for the first time in three years to reach the magic 30 home runs and 30 steals, but he didn't miss by much—29 home runs, 31 steals. He led the league in runs scored and stolen bases. He led his own club in hitting, home runs, triples, base hits, and runs batted in.

You cannot break into a new city with more than that, unless you bring money. But it wasn't enough, and from the start there has been a slight edginess between Mays and his fans. Less so now that the city has come to understand Mays and baseball better, but it's still there.

It began right away, too. There were 23,448 fans in pleasantly intimate Seals Stadium on the afternoon of April 15, 1958—Opening Day, the Dodgers against the Giants. Three thousand miles had passed, but they were still the Dodgers and the Giants. As a matter of fact, the flavor of the rivalry had changed little. Los Angeles was the new Brooklyn, a loud-mouthed, brash and flashy town, like its predecessor riddled by inferiority complexes. San Francisco was the new Manhattan—cool, sophisticated, witty, urbane, understandably proud. There are basic differences, however. Los Angeles fans are ignorant; Brooklyn fans were shrewd. San Francisco fans are equally ignorant; New York Giant fans were the smartest in baseball.

Playing that first day under what one San Francisco baseball writer called "nursery-blue skies," the Giants won the West Coast premiere, 8-0. Willie Mays had two hits. They were infield hits, however, although one of them nearly removed Charley Neal's hand. And on that first day it was decided that Mays wasn't as good as a local boy named Joe DiMaggio.

San Francisco had not expected much from this 1958 Giant team. It had expected much from Mays. To the astonishment of all baseball, a Giant team bristling with rookies caught the town's fancy, made a strong run for three-and-a-half months, led the league for a spell (or until Casey Stengel said they were "freaks") and finished a happy third. It was a new, young team, and it ran bases as hard (now I wonder who taught them that?) as any team since the Gashouse Gang of the 1930's. Not as well as the Cards ran (except for Mays who ran better than Pepper Martin) but as hard; sometimes they ran into each other, piled two and three men on the same base, overslid bases, forgot to touch others. The first Giant loss to Los Angeles that year resulted from young Jim Davenport's forgetting to touch third on his way home. Jim wept, and the fans loved him even more.

And Mays? His .347 (second by three points to Richie Ashburn—Mays needed five hits the last game to win the title, and he got only three) wasn't enough. He had come with too glowing a record. San Franciscans are not used to hyperbole. They disdain the uses of press agentry. If somebody has said Willie Mays is ten feet nine inches tall, San Franciscans carefully expect a man three inches shy of 11 feet, and not a hair shorter. In Los Angeles they would have gawked at Mays, whipped out the tape measure, and said he was easily 11 feet, and maybe 12.

In truth, the fans had something to kick about. Willie Mays suffers from periodic slumps; everybody knows this. In 1958 he had one of the worst slumps of his career, a near two-month drought in midseason. Day after day the boxscore read 0-for-4, 0-for-3, 1-for-5. He stopped hitting home runs; he stopped driving in runs. He tried changing his stance. Nothing availed. The Giants lost four ball games in Milwaukee, end of July, beginning of August—to end their pennant hopes—and time after time it was Mays killing rallies.

The slump was so bad that they sent Willie to a hospital back East to see if something basic was ailing. (The next day Willie got three hits and stole three bases, and now he goes to a hospital every so often for a day or two.)

When Mays wound up with a .347 average, one question had to be posed: Can you imagine what Mays would have hit if he hadn't had his two-month slump?

The slump was more pronounced to outsiders reading the boxscores than it was to the Giants themselves. In early August, right after the Milwaukee debacle, I asked Bill Rigney about Mays.

"He carried us a whole month, all by himself," Rigney said.

"But what about the slump?"

Rigney looked blank. "That's what everybody keeps saying. That he hasn't hit a home run in so many days or knocked in a run in a hundred or so times at bat. Maybe I'm too close. Maybe I don't see things like that. But I know this: Mays is having a helluva year, even for him. The things he does!"

Jim Hegan, who had seen too much of Mays in the 1954 Series when Hegan was the Indian catcher, found himself in the National League in 1958. The first time he played against the Giants, Hegan hit a ball into left-centerfield that Mays one-handed, robbing Hegan of his first National League hit. Later in the game, with runners on first and second, Hegan dropped a looping fly ball into short center and skipped into first base thinking that he had himself a hit, only to learn that Mays had come tearing in to trap the ball and fire to third for a force out. (Hegan quickly left the league and found easier work as a Yankee bullpen coach.)

But that was in the field and besides, Mays seemed to save his best plays for the road. In a small park such as Seals Stadium making great catches is like making catches in a phone booth. In Candlestick Park making great catches is like making them in a tornado. Mays had also hit better on the road most San Francisco years—another reason eleven cities think Mays *is* Superman, or at least an Apollo Moonwalker. He does have slumps; nearly all great hitters do, from Cobb to Clemente. Willie's slumps nearly always follow a hot streak. In 1958 there was one stretch, also at home, when Mays was on base 11 times straight. Fans started to expect more and more. ("They're never going to get him out.") Mays himself says, completely without conceit, "When I'm going good, they's nothing they can do, excep' walk me."

Then it gets cold. One for 21. The Mays slumps are intriguing. He has had some grand ones, too, like his first 22 times at bat in Trenton, his one-for-26 with the Giants when he first came up in 1951, his long drought in June and July of 1958, the first year in Frisco, and the slump that lasted over three months in the second half of the 1964 season. There have been other, less dramatic slumps. He had a "poor" season in 1956, with lots of brief hitless streaks, but none of them too obvious because he just never got off the ground in 1956. (If you want to call the years 1956 and 1964 slump years—both years he hit .296—there are an even dozen hitters in the Hall of Fame who would swap their lifetime batting averages for a .296, including Joe Tinker, that peerless shortstop who not only couldn't make the double play but also hit a rousing lifetime .264.)

Once I asked Willie Mays' opinion of his slumps.

"Playing 150 games like I do is very strenuous," Mays said. "Every June or July when it gets hot, I get tired and I go into a slump. But then when it cools off a little in September or maybe after I rest a day or two, I hit again. I am what you call a late comer."

"How come you didn't hit too well in September of '60?" (A question like that is very revealing: Mays hit about .315 that month.)

"Because we had four days off in a row," he said. "I lost my touch. That was too long a rest."

The slump. There is something at work besides physical agents, stances and July heat or fatigue. (And besides the chill and wind in San Francisco. When Mays and the Giants moved out West, Willie appeared on a Bob Hope television program, and Hope asked him about the San Francisco weather. "It's not bad when you can see it through the fog," joshed Willie. In fact, few athletes operate as well in cold, windy weather as they do in warm sunshine and no wind.)

The slumps may be summed up (but not entirely) with the word "first." First licks in Trenton, first licks in the National League, first licks in a World Series, first season in San Francisco. Some sort of pressure stemming from newness gets to Mays. But it is not only or always that. When Mays goes off on a week-long batting spree, as he does so often, another sort of pressure must start to build—a slow-starting but nagging doubt: *Can I be this good? Can anybody?* If you watch Mays closely during one of his base-hit binges, he is almost careless at the plate, grabbing the bat and jumping in, standing any which way, and clouting the first pitch out of sight. I remember an exhibition game in Palm Springs against the Los Angeles Angels, when Mays was having a week of hits. The Angel pitcher threw wildly, right at the top of Mays' head, and Willie started to fall, holding his bat like a hatchet. On his way down he decided *whatthehell* and with his hatchet-bat clubbed at the ball. It shot into the left-field corner for a two-base hit.

So much for the slump. If fatigue is the reason, resting seems to be the antidote. If fatigue isn't the reason, whatever it is will remain a secret. "I'm the only one who knows what's in here," Willie has said, tapping his heart. Perhaps it pertains to slumps as well as to women.

In 1959 the San Francisco Giants should have won the pennant. In 1958 they had been too green and their pitching too thin, the staff completing just 41 games all year. So they got a year older picked up Sam Jones and Jack Sanford to stouten the pitching.

They didn't win, as all the civilized world and Los Angeles knows. They lost by three ball games when they dropped seven of their last eight (.500 ball would have tied; anything better would have won), but the 1959 pennant should have been out of reach before that. The Giants didn't lose the pennant that last week; they lost it in early June when Jack Sanford broke his hand and was out nearly a month and in mid-August when Jim Davenport hurt his leg and was out over a month. Had Sanford been around, they might have picked up the necessary three or four wins right there. At third, Davenport was saving a game a week, it seemed, in '59. The two losses probably meant six or seven games.

In 1959 Mays hit .313. He hit five more home runs than he had in 1958, he drove in eight more runs (104), and for the third time he exceeded Mel Ott's old Giant record of 81 extra-base hits. For the fourth year in a row Mays led the league in steals and, also for the fourth year in a row, had 25 or more steals (27) to go with his 25 or more home runs (34).

He did this despite his being plagued with a rash of injuries: a gashed leg that required 35 stitches in spring training (that Mays says cost him a month getting fit); a fractured finger; a sore thigh; a recurring shoulder ache; a bad back. The streakiness was less noticeable and the list of clutch hits too long to recount in full. Here is a sample:

On April 18, Mays took special batting practice to get out of an early slump. Then he hit two home runs in an 8-1 win over St. Louis. The next day he drove in two runs against St. Louis, and the Giants won by those two runs. On May 2, the Giants took the league lead; Mays had four singles in an 8-5 win over the Braves. On June 11, Mays came off the bench nursing a bad back, the Giants trailing by two, and hit a three-run pinch home-run off unbeaten Roy Face. (The Giants went on to lose.) On July 5, the Giants beat the Cards by two runs. Mays had a two-run home run. On July 18, the Giants beat the Pirates, 4-3, on Mays' two-run home run in the eighth.

It went that way right on through the mid-season heat into August, and on August 7, in San Francisco,

Mays jammed the second joint of a finger on his right hand while sliding back to first on a vain pick-off play. The finger hurt Mays, but he stayed in and had two singles and a double. One of the singles, with two out in the ninth, won the ball game, 3-2.

Mays sat out the game of August 8 (he explained vaguely that his hand had been hurt), except to strike out in a pinch-hitting role. The next day he sat on the bench until the eighth inning, when he hit a pinch single and scored the tying run in a game that the Giants won, 4-3, in the tenth. The Giants were nursing a lead that seesawed from a game to three games, and the pressure was on as they met the Braves and the Dodgers.

So Mays took his injured finger into action on August 10, and with the Giants trailing St. Louis, 2-0, going into the ninth, Mays singled off Larry Jackson (to drive him from the box) and cut the lead to 2-1, sending the tying run to third. Minutes later, Kirkland doubled and the Giants had won, 3-2.

The next day Mays hit a double in the tenth inning of a 4-4 game, and his prancing off base so worried Lindy McDaniel (delighted later to be a Giant) that the relief ace wild-pitched and Mays moved to third. With a drawn-in infield, Kirkland hit a sharp groundball past Stan Musial at first, and the Giants had won another heartstopper. The headlines read, "Kirkland Comes Through Again," which was true enough, except that Mays had made it possible.

Two days later the Giants were massacred 20-9 by the Cubs, but Mays kept at it with a triple and a home run in three at-bats. Two days after that, he had a single and a home run to drive in two runs and score three in a 6-4 win over the Cubs.

The next day, August 16, the Giants lost, 5-4, but you couldn't blame Mays. He hit a home run with a man on, plus a single, and stole one base. The lead was two-and-a-half games over the Dodgers and three-and-a-half over Milwaukee. The next day Davenport crashed into Ed Bailey at the plate and was carried off.

On the 20th Mays had three hits at Milwaukee in a 5-3 win. Warren Spahn was the pitcher. On August 21 the Giants won two games in Philadelphia, and in the city of Quaker serenity Mays drove the usually unruffled and gentlemanly Philadelphia pitcher Robin Roberts right out of his mind. It was the sixth inning of the first game of the twinighter; Mays was standing on second base. The reason he was standing there instead of taking his usual long jitterfoot lead was that Roberts was holding the ball, head cocked over his right shoulder, while the Giants' Daryl Spencer waited at the plate for a pitch that obviously wouldn't be thrown until Roberts was dead certain that Mays would stay put.

Mays waved his arms and yelled to Spencer to step out of the box, to break the tableau and make Roberts begin his stretch delivery all over, to give Mays a chance to dance his few worrisome steps toward third.

Now Robin Roberts had been around. He had been around 12 years as of this date in 1959. He had gone through such nerve-fluttering moments with Jackie Robinson in Robinson's absolute daredevil prime, and Roberts had never before flipped. He had

matched wits and balk motions with such runners as
Sam Jethroe, Bill Bruton, and Johnny Temple. You
do what you can: fake the man back to second, wag
your head at him, step off the mound and throw or
don't, and usually end up simply by mopping your
brow, which is the reason ball games take two hours
and fifty minutes. Meanwhile the runner has his little
arsenal. He leads off, fakes a break, ducks back, and
goes down or doesn't go down. He must keep an eye
on the shortstop and second baseman, or just one
while the third-base coach watches the other, and he
eyes the pitcher as he goes into his little stretch.

It is a battle that has occupied National League
pitchers and runners for a century now. Finally,
something must happen; the pitcher must eventually
throw the ball somewhere.

Not so this time. Robin Roberts, then the prince of
all pitchers, suddenly called "Time!" to the plate
umpire and walked toward Mays snapping angry
words at the Giant baserunner. Umpire Jocko Conlan,
a man seldom to be upstaged, stepped between the
irate Roberts and the baffled Mays, and pretty soon
Roberts was led back to the mound, from which
location he finally made his pitch to Spencer.

When it was all over, and the game had been won
by the Giants, 6-0, and the second game as well,
Roberts explained his aberration:

"It was an impulsive thing to do, an immature
thing. I don't know why I did it, but I accused Willie
of stealing the catcher's signs. I heard him yelling out
there and moving around and I just went out to tell
him about it . . ."

It *was* impulsive, immature, and foolish. Even if it were true that Mays had been stealing signs, there is little Roberts could do about it except ask for a catcher with shorter fingers. It all adds up to the staggering truth that Mays had temporarily driven steady old Robin Roberts out of his mind.

Oh, yes. On that pitch to Spencer, Mays stole third.

So even when Mays wasn't hitting—he went hitless the first game of the doubleheader—he was still upsetting the foe. It didn't always work. On August 27, the Giants played another doubleheader in Philadelphia and lost both ends this time. A Mays home run in the second game off Don Cardwell put the Giants ahead, but it wasn't enough. The next night Mays went three-for-four against the Dodgers, drove in three runs and made two great plays in the field. This was also the day Mays told announcer Vin Scully that baseball was a business. (He failed to add that it was hard to see the joy in a game, playing with a broken finger for 20 days.)

On August 30 Mays homered for the third game in a row, scored two runs and drove in two, but the Giants lost to Los Angeles, 7-6. The pressure was becoming almost too much for players and fans alike, but the drumfire kept sounding from Mays' bat. His three-run home run—his 25th—on September 3 beat the Cubs, 8-5. Two days later his home run beat the Cards, 3-2. Four days later it wasn't his bat, but Mays wasn't still: he scored from second on a force out and the Giants beat Pittsburgh. A reporter, shaking hands with Mays in the dressing room, noticed him wince, and Mays finally talked about the broken finger and told the reporter not to let it out. It was headlines the next day, and there was this Mays quote:

"I can't swing right. I've been throwing myself at the ball. But I don't want anybody knowing about it. I don't want anybody to think I'm setting up an alibi. I haven't seen a doctor. I can help the club in the field, even if I haven't been helping them much at bat. I know the old man (Stoneham) wouldn't want me to play and that man has been as good to me as any man I've ever known. If they put the finger in a cast, I wouldn't be able to play."

The same day Mays hit two home runs. This was September 10. Of the team's last 17 home runs eight were Mays'. He had hit 11 home runs since breaking his finger just over a month ago. Before the season ended, he would hit five more. The Giants led by one after the game of August 11, Roberts shutting them out, 1-0; Mays had the only extra-base hit, a double, and he made a superb catch of a ball hit by Joe Koppe to keep the game within reach.

On September 15 Mays went two-for-four, including a home run. The next day he had two doubles. And on September 17, before the unbelieving folk at San Francisco, Mays had his greatest day of the year. He had four hits in four trips, including a home run. He also walked once. He scored two runs and drove in five. The Giants had beaten Milwaukee, 13-6. They went crazy over Willie that day; they cheered him; they loved him.

And during the next two days, while Los Angeles, with the hottest pitching staff in the majors, was throttling the Giants three straight and the Giant lead disappeared for good, the fans got on Willie and booed him. Not much, but enough to be heard. In the three-game set with Los Angeles he had three hits in ten trips, for a puny .300.

That left the Giants tied for the lead, but everybody knew they were through, Charley Dressen chortling again: "The Giants is dead, the Giants is dead," and nearly everybody quitting. Not Mays. Willie hit like a fiend those last five days, carrying a dead ball club into Chicago and St. Louis. Ten hits in 18 trips. Three home runs. Two doubles. But the Giants lost four of those five, and the season was over.

Somebody figured it out. From September 12th, when the Giants were leading by one, until the season's end Willie Mays had hit .460.

Willie kept his bargain with a barnstorming team, played a couple of games, and then when the tour hit New York, checked into the New York City Medical Center to have his broken finger treated.

By the end of 1959 it was generally agreed that the Giants needed still more pitching and more defense. They traded for a fine second baseman, Don Blasingame, and got pitcher Billy O'Dell and humorist Billy Loes. Then Willie Mays said, "That looks good, but we need a bench, too," and the Giants went out and bought Dave Philley, Dale Long, and Jim Marshall.

When 1960 opened at new Candlestick Park on the Bay, Governor Edmund G. (Pat) Brown stood there (with his hands in his overcoat pockets, it was that cold) and said he hoped the Giants would get together with the Dodgers in the World Series, and Dick

Nixon said he hoped the Giants would, like any good politician, come up strong in November, and that sums up what Brown and Nixon know about baseball.

Then the games started. It was April 12, and Sam Jones beat the Cards, 3-1, before 42,269 in the packed $15-million park, and everybody laughed embarrassedly because the wind was so much stronger than anybody had expected and the radiant heating under the seats didn't work. And when Jeff Carter, the Giants' public-address announcer said, "License number such-and-so, your boat is adrift," the crowd roared with happy laughter. Nobody knew how symbolic Carter's words were.

Chapter Twelve

A man has to be a masochist or a Dodger fan to spend much time on the 1960 San Francisco Giants. There have been disappointing Giant teams in the past. The 1934 Giants blew a pennant they should have won. 1958 was the year of hot rookies and false hopes, followed by 1959, when the front-running Giants gradually fell apart. Later, in 1965, the Giants trailed, got hot and then cooled off, and the Dodgers won.

This 1960 season remains a memory of dropped pop flies, stupid baserunning, futile hitting, ineffective spot pitching, and incomprehensible, reprehensible managing, buried beneath jeers and laughter, all on display in a beautiful new ball park. Even this was a mistake. Candlestick Park sits on a jut of forlorn land where the smell of clams and polluted water is thicker than Los Angeles smog and fouler than Canarsie garbage.

There are nice roomy lockers in the dressing rooms at Candlestick Park, and the floors are carpeted. The seats are of a special unpainted cypress. Pipes under the stands heat the pavement and then your toes and maybe even your seats. Except they didn't work. Before the season was over, Stoneham was being sued by San Francisco's king of damage suits, lawyer Melvin

Belli, a season boxseat holder who was asking damages for nearly freezing his toes. And when Mr. Belli—who fished the Alaskan creeks, clad in his BVDs, his only weapon a bottle of Jim Beam—freezes his feet, it's got to be cold.

Belli won his suit for $1,597 and used the money to plant Lombardy poplars in the street. Belli called the decision "a mandate to the Giants to keep the fires burning." But the cold had set in, and the Giants seemed headed for another long winter of winless years. In 1959 they had come close. In 1960 they fell apart. Was this to be the future?

If it was, Willie Mays would not respect it. He hit .319 in 1960, third best in the league, trailing Dick Groat by six points and Norm Larker by four. He hit 29 home runs; he drove in 103 runs. Larker and Groat had seven home runs between them. Together they had 65 extra-base hits. Mays had 70.

The source of Mays' trouble is evident. He hit .299 in San Francisco and a rousing .338 on the road. He had 12 home runs at home and 17 away.

The wind, she blew—from left and out to right— and Mays had to shift his feet to hit every ball down the rightfield line. On the road, he had to rearrange himself again. Wally Moon said that balls hit to left field acted as if they were on rubber bands. They just stopped in mid-air and bounced back to the infield. Don Blasingame said the wind made popfly hitters out of strong right-handed batters. (This didn't explain why it also made a popfly hitter out of linedriving left-handed Don Blasingame.) Charley Dressen wanted to know how much it would cost to put a dome on top, and everybody laughed; nobody puts domes on ball fields. Dressen complained that the wind even affected pitched balls and made it hard for the umpires to follow them—the first time Dressen had admitted that umpires ever did follow pitches. The Giants' Jim Marshall suggested starting games at eight in the morning because it wasn't so windy then (just foggy).

The Giants were assured that the wind would die down in June. On June 11, 1960, Orlando Cepeda, after being called out on strikes, threw his helmet in the air, and the wind carried it ten rows into the seats.

On June 1, the Giants beat the Cubs, 2-1, the kind of tight, low-hit contest a true Giant fan loves winning. Rigney, instead of exulting, fretted, "We can't seem to get even a good pop."

Three days later the Giants played a game so nearly perfect it drove poor Rigney crazy. Jack Sanford pitched a three-hit shutout (his third of the season, and the Giants' tenth in 46 games). The Giants themselves made only three hits, but—and this is what is so perfect—they bunched them all in the third inning, two singles and a double, and scored twice. They didn't leave a man on base all day. So Rigney chewed his knuckles and two days later benched McCovey *and* Cepeda, both for not hitting. This left him without a first baseman of any stature.

Then there was Clancy. Tom Sheehan used to be a hotel private detective. He is also a former Philly pitcher who one year posted a 1-and-17 record. With these credentials he was given a disheartened, descending club. Whatever chance Clancy Sheehan had was scrapped when Stoneham said at the time of hiring, "Sheehan's my manager, for two or three weeks, or possibly the whole season."

The Giant front office is astonishingly frank when it comes to the future of its managers. In September, 1964, not long after Alvin Dark had been quoted as downgrading the mentality of Latin and Negro ballplayers, the Giants' general manager, Charles (Chub) Feeney—Horace Stoneham's nephew—said in the pressbox of Philadelphia's Connie Mack Stadium, "When a manager has lost the confidence of his players, he has lost his value to the team." He said no more; he did not have to. Alvin Dark was through and the press knew it. Three weeks later it was official.

In 1960 the Giants knew they had a lame-duck manager, because Horace Stoneham had candidly said as much. So they ran all over Clancy. They broke curfew and played cards all night, sometimes passing $100 on the turn of a card in blackjack. Sheehan had to fine Jack Sanford $200 for walking off the mound without waiting for the formal relief call. McCovey was overweight. Eddie Bressoud failed to chase a fly pop by Frank Thomas, and Willie Mays trotted on a fly ball to the same Thomas, which landed behind Frank.

Injuries. Mays had a cold, the flu and another jammed finger. Hobie Landrith broke a hand in spring training. Antonelli had a recurring muscle spasm and would never pitch well again. Davenport's knee was never fully healed; then he got plunked on the collar bone by a Larry Jackson pitch, and finally he began to vomit blood in a Milwaukee hotel room because he didn't know he had a gastric ulcer. He was out a month and two days. Cepeda, hit on the head with a thrown ball by Maury Wills, was out a week. McCovey, Bressoud and Marichal were all hurt at one time or other.

In the field it was one huge error. In the fifth inning of the April 29 game against the Dodgers, the Giants gave their foes eight outs and eight unearned runs. The Giants led, 2-1, behind Sam Jones, when Norm Larker punched a hit to center to open the fifth. Maury Wills ripped a line drive to Joe Amalfitano at third who gloved it, then dropped it. The scorer called it a hit, so this is not one of the eight outs. John Podres bunted to move up the runners, but when Jones fell down fielding it, it went for a hit. This is not among the eight outs either. (If you figure Amalfitano would have had a double play had he held the Wills shot, then the Giants gave the Dodgers 11 outs.) With the bases now loaded, Jones threw to Jim Gilliam, who hit a one-bouncer back to Jones. With an easy double play in front of him Jones threw the ball past catcher Bob Schmidt and then, instead of covering the plate, turned his back in disgust. Not only did Larker score; Wills came in too.

Charley Neal hit a one-bouncer to shortstop Bressoud, and with another double play in sight, Bressoud fumbled the ball. The bases were filled again, and still nobody was out. Moon hit a one-bouncer to McCovey, playing in on the grass. Hoping for a force at the plate and perhaps a doubleplay back to first, McCovey fired past Schmidt. Later, John Roseboro hit a 3-2 pitch for a bases-loaded home run. Why not?

Yet in 1960 Willie Mays never put out more. Take the doubleheader of May 30, 1960, at Candlestick Park. It was a staggering display of baseball virtuosity. The Giants split with the Cubs that day. In the first game, which the Giants lost 2-1, Mays went one for three, stole a base, scored the Giants' only run, and made two spectacular catches, once robbing Ernie Banks of an extra-base hit and again one-handing Ed Bouchee's low liner in right-centerfield after a long sprint. There were some witnesses who considered the catch on Bouchee the greatest they had ever seen.

In the second contest, Willie stole two more bases, drove in two runs with a home run, had a second hit, and scored two runs. Best of all, in the ninth, Mays worked Cub pitcher Seth Morehead for a walk with one out. Willie McCovey hit a ground ball between first and second into right field, and Mays sped merrily around to third base. Rightfielder Bob Will—with a powerful arm—saw that he had no play on Mays, so he nonchalantly threw the ball to Jerry Kindall, then the Cub second baseman, to drive McCovey back to first.

And Mays, running with his head over his shoulders, saw the nonchalant toss and continued right on running to score all the way from first on a routine single. The Giants won, 5-4.

Mays joshed about it later: "It was getting cold out there on the bases."

Mays scored twice from first on singles in 1960; neither time was he running with the pitch. Each time the Giants won by a single run. Most men never score from first on a single; for years, Mays did it every season.

On the second day of the season Mays went four-for-five, including the first bunt hit of his career. He made two other bunt hits in 1960, to win a $15 necktie from Russ Hodges who bet Mays he wouldn't bunt safely three times all year.

The first bunt had the usual repercussions. Once on first, Mays stole second. Then Ernie Broglio tried to pick him off and threw the ball away, whereupon Mays took third, to score on a pinch single by Cepeda.

On June 24 in Cincinnati, while snapping a five-game losing streak, Mays hit two home runs and a single, stole home, and made ten put-outs in centerfield, two shy of the all-time record. In an 11-inning game in Philadelphia, he had three triples and two other hits. The third triple drove in the lead run; Mays scored it on a sacrifice fly. In another game Mays had two triples. Five triples in two separate games, or more triples than the average player hits all year.

Just before another game with the Phils, Sheehan blasted his wayward boys for curfew violations and too many high-stake card games. Mays, who was not one of the offenders, went out and had a four-for-four night (a homer, a triple and two singles), scored three runs, drove in four, stole a base, and led the Boy Scouts to an 11-5 win.

Mays hit one grand-slam home run in 1960, on

August 25 against the Reds, and the Giants won by three.

On June 30, the day Dick Stuart hogged the headlines with three home runs and a single in the second game of a doubleheader (Giants 11-0, Pirates 11-6), Mays hit a home run in each game and two doubles, a triple and a single, for five runs-batted-in and a six-for-seven day. Stuart had 13 bases that day; Mays had 16.

June put the Mays slump and the Mays streak side by side. Early that month, Mays had one single in 20 trips. Then he went on a tear, beginning with a night game in San Francisco on June 10. Mays had three-for-three that night, two singles and a 410-foot home run with two on, and he stole two bases. Spahn (yawn) was the pitcher.

This set off a 12-game streak in which Mays hit .420. In the twelve games he had six home runs, a triple, and five doubles. He drove in 16 runs and scored 15.

So that was the 1960 season, the Giants a bedraggled crew and Willie Mays shining as brightly as ever before. It marked the beginning of a new decade and more or less the end of Mays' first decade in big-league baseball. Early in the 1961 season he would celebrate his tenth anniversary with the Giants, on May 6, his thirtieth birthday. There seemed little more that Willie Mays, now a mature man, could show us.

How wrong can you be? On Tuesday, April 25, 1961, Willie and his Giants came to Los Angeles to

play the Dodgers. Mays was having a Mays beginning; he had hit two home runs, both at Candlestick
and both into the left-field seats. They were the only
home runs, day or night, that had been hit into left
field in April in San Francisco. Mays had stolen three
bases. He was hitting .320.

In the seventh inning of a superb ball game between these two clubs that somehow manage to level
the odds to dead-even whenever they meet, Mays
reached back ten years for his magic. The Giants led,
3-1, but the Dodgers had filled the bases with one out,
and Wally Moon, then the hottest hitter in baseball,
up there. The man on third was Maury Wills, who
had stolen 50 bases the year before.

Stu Miller, in relief of Jack Sanford, tossed up a
dead fish, and Moon hit it on the nose, to centerfield.
Mays came rushing up on the ball, but the line drive
was doing tricks, tailing off to Mays' right like a
golfer's dying slice. Mays had to lunge to make the
catch, but he grabbed it, he drew back his right arm
and let fly.

Down the line came Wills, running a mere 90 feet
on perhaps the fastest legs in all of baseball then.
Behind him came a baseball travelling 300-plus feet.
Tom Haller, who has played football at the University of Illinois, took the throw standing an inch in
front of home, and Wills was effectively blocked off.
It wasn't close; the throw was not to be believed.
Mays himself said slowly, after some thought, "No, I
don't know if I could ever do it again." (Four years
later he made his 406-foot throw in Forbes Field, and
a few months after that a throw nearly identical to

this one against the Dodgers—again with Wills the runner, but this time Haller did not quite block off Wills, and the runner scored.)

The Giants held on grimly that night in 1961, to win 3-1 and move into first place. The great play on Furillo and Cox in 1951—in a game the Giants also won, 3-1—had found its mate a decade later.

Five afternoons later, on Sunday, April 30, before 13,114 astonished citizens at Milwaukee's County Stadium, Mays hit four home runs in a single game. The home-run jag broke a small slump just getting underway. Friday night, Warren Spahn threw a no-hitter against the Giants, and Mays went hitless—naturally—in three trips. But what was worse, Spahn noted that Willie was "swinging badly," and Mays agreed. Willie struck out twice that night against a pitcher who was having the greatest night of his career, but who always had trouble not merely getting Mays out but keeping himself alive.

Still, it was a no-hitter, and Mays was doing what the rest of the boys were doing—nothing. The next day was far more serious. In clobbering Milwaukee, the Giants hit five home runs and ten other hits, but Mays went 0-for-4. During a seven-trip streak Mays' average was below .300. Giant officials squirmed and looked at the calendar, hoping Mays would come out of it before June 15.

The next day was It. "The greatest day I've ever had," Willie called it. It was appropriately game number 1234 in Mays' career, and that's what he hit—1,2,3, and 4, all in one game. A home run off Lew Burdette in the first, nobody on. A home run off

Burdette in the third, one on. A home run off Seth Morehead in the sixth, two on. A home run off Don McMahon in the eighth, one on. There was some small sense of retribution in this fourth home run. Back in 1958, when the front-running Giants moved into Milwaukee in late July, the Braves had swept a four-game series. It was Mays' striking out against Don McMahon with men on base that spoiled a rally in one of the games.

On this last day of April, 1961, Willie drove in eight runs. They got him out once, in the fifth inning. Moe Drabowsky pulled it off; all Willie did was hit a line shot to dead centerfield. Had he got some loft to the ball, it would have meant five, not four, home runs.

Four is enough. With them, Mays joined eight other major-league hitters: Bobby Lowe, Ed Delahanty, Lou Gehrig, Chuck Klein, Pat Seerey, Gill Hodges, Joe Adcock, and Rocky Colavito. Seerey and Klein got theirs in extra-inning games. Only nine times has the four-in-one game been accomplished. Compare this with the 150 or so no-hitters and you see the staggering magnitude of Mays' deed.

Six days later Willie Mays became thirty years old.

His greatness had been attested to by a solid phalanx of opinion. Bill Corum had called him the greatest fielder the game ever saw; Dan Daniel had called him the greatest thrower. Sportswriter Milton Gross, a long-time Mays student, had declared, "Hands down, the greatest all-round player in the game today."

Bobby Bragan had said that Mays could have been

the National League all-star second baseman, short-stop, or third-baseman any season, had he decided to be an infielder. And Bill Rigney had remarked, "Willie can run and throw and catch better than anyone who ever lived."

But it took Leo Durocher to put it in terms that seem more Maysian:

"Willie is without doubt the most dynamic, most dramatic, most fantastic, most exciting performer in action today. He is Joe Louis, Jascha Heifetz, Sammy Davis, and Nashua rolled into one."

So a man becomes thirty. Mays said that year:

"I don't drive cars too fast any more . . . You value life more, as you get older. The same with that stick-ball. You get hurt in the street, you're thirty years old, you can't recover as fast. The big difference is that now I know *how* to play better. I don't say I *can* play better, but I know how. I am more wiser. When I came up, Alvin Dark had to signal behind his back to me on every pitch for every hitter, tell me where to play. I didn't know nothing then."

In 1965 Mays did the signalling, telling young infielders what to do, moving his fellow outfielders. On days he did not play, he sat in the outfield bullpen and wigwagged the outfielders from there. He arranged with young Hal Lanier, the fine Giant infielder, when to go to the mound and talk to a pitcher, just to give the man in the bullpen more time to warm up. Then—in 1951—he knew nothing, he says. Now, nearly two decades later, he knows how the game is to be played. In 1966, after he'd broken Jimmy Foxx's home-run mark, Mays was asked whether he'd ever want to manage a ball club. "I don't want to think of things like managing," he answered. "I got enough to think about playing. But in my mind there ain't any job I can't do on a baseball field."

He spoke—back in 1961—of the pitchers. He divided them into two groups, the men who threw the ball and "the competitors." Don Drysdale, he said, was a competitor. He named some others. And he admitted, as candidly as a ballplayer ever has admitted these things, "I'd rather not have to face them. The competitors. Not 'cause they throw at me. They just competitors. Sometimes you feel: 'This guy I can't hit.' Other times you know they can't get you out. I do everything in streaks. I'm a funny guy. One time a pitch gets me out. Next time I hit it. All my life, I've had those spells, hot and cold. If I'm hitting the long ball, I keep trying to hit it. I even steal in streaks."

In March, 1961, when I spoke with Mays in Arizona, he had ahead of him another season, another half-year of travelling around the nation.

"When I'm on the road, I like to sleep late. Maybe 'til nine. Then I order breakfast in my room. Then maybe I go back to sleep a while. Sleep and breakfast are the most important things to me, keeping me strong. I'm a funny guy. I'd rather play night games. At night I am, what you say, more wide awake. Daytime, I feel logey. When I'm free I take in lots of movies. Westerns, lots of fighting. I like action. On the road, I get to the park for a night game around six, and I'm ready for batting practice by 7:15. If I have friends in the town—like in Chicago—I might spend an hour with them. I like to get back to the hotel early after the game. I don't smoke, I don't drink, I don't get involved in big-stake games, or breaking curfew.

"On the road I take along a small tape recorder. I used to carry a portable phonograph, but it was too heavy. I picked up the tape recorder in Japan, during the trip last winter. Had a terrible time in Japan. I was sick most of the time. The climate or something, I guess. My gums were all swole up and my stomach was upset."

He must have had a terrible time. He hit .390 during the Japanese trip, with eight home runs. Mays was judged the most valuable player of the tour.

"I won a car, a Japanese car. A Datsun Bluebird."

But the trip wasn't as artistically successful as other major-league tours of Japan. The Giants lost a few ball games, and had to fight for others. It may have been a stubborn carry-over from the dreary 1960 National League campaign.

"I don't want to talk about 1960," Mays said. "A bad year. I don't like to dig up the past. Let it rest."

Some moments of it remain pleasantly vivid, however, such as a catch that he said he prized above all others. Now when Mays makes a great catch, he will say, "I can't say whether it was better or worse than other catches. That's not for me to say. That's for you people to say. You saw them, you decide." But in 1961, he said:

"The best play I ever made was in Brooklyn, against Bobby Morgan. Not the Wertz catch. That was a money play, like they said, and the throw was the most important part. Not the catch on Skinner or the one on Clemente [this was a barehanded grab in deep left-center] or on Burton or on anybody. This one in Ebbets Field on Morgan is the one I remember best. It was the last of the ninth, two on, and the score tied. He hit it into left center, to my right, and it would have hit the wall about belt high. I ran over and jumped so I was stretched straight out, and I caught the ball with my fingertips and then when I fell my right elbow jammed into my stomach and knocked me out. Leo came out and rolled me over, and I was still holding the ball. We lost the game in the tenth."

That was Mays before the 1961 season, selecting the bright spots of the past. And during the season he had his great days—the four home runs in a single game, for example. Yet that season there was a gray quality to what Mays did, as if he felt that the age of thirty had meaning and that what followed might be downhill. At the All-Star break, his marriage officially collapsed, Willie Mays was in debt, owing money he hadn't yet earned but had received from the Giants. He also owed the federal government thousands of dollars in back taxes.

In Arizona a few months before his marriage officially died, Mays told me that he and his business advisors were looking for some kind of business he could invest in, something to tide him over in future years.

These are the weights he carried into 1961. Yet he hit .308. He hammered out 40 home runs; not since

WILLIE MAYS

1955 had he hit so many. He drove in a towering 123 runs and led the league with 129 runs scored. Under new manager Alvin Dark, the team was third, with 85 wins, the most games a Giant team had won since the powerhouse of 1954, and Mays was the key to the team's rebounding.

So a man would waver, looking at Mays in 1961. Would 1962 be a new beginning for this astonishing ballplayer? Or were we witnessing the start of the end?

That winter I wrote an article for a magazine, and I titled it: Is Willie Mays Headed for Disaster? The editor of the magazine changed the title on the cover to WILLIE MAYS IS HEADED FOR DISASTER.

Like winning a pennant the next season. Like leading the league in home runs then and twice more in the next three years. Like being selected overwhelmingly to each All-Star game. Like being selected the Most Valuable Player in his league in 1965.

We should all have such disasters.

Chapter Thirteen

With the first swing of his bat in the 1962 season Willie Mays hit a home run, and the Giants belted Milwaukee, 6-0, behind Juan Marichal.

One home run does not make a season, but if you were waiting to bury Willie Mays because of a busted marriage and a few misspent dollars, you waited in vain. And perhaps that opening day home run—off Warren Spahn, of course—was an early tip-off.

This was the year of expansion in the National League. The new teams in New York and Houston frankly did not make the league any better, but they did make for more fun. Any National League team in New York has to add to the zest of baseball. And when the team is managed by Casey Stengel, well, how much more zest can you get? As for Houston, its approach to the competition was more staid. It built its team with youth and put it under the shrewd handling of baseball's smartest (if least inspirational) field manager, Paul Richards. Later, when Houston moved under the Dome and the game became a spectacle, Richards was no longer needed. But now, in the beginning, the tall, lean, wily Texan who had hit a rousing .227 in his major-league career was the right man for the building job.

Still, the season soon eliminated the Mets and

Houston from the real competition. They were there simply to fill out the schedule and to make some money. So were six other teams. What it got down to was another harrowing contest between the Giants and the Dodgers.

It should not have been that close. Had not Sandy Koufax hurt the index finger of his pitching hand and been lost to the Dodgers for nearly half a season, the Giants could not have caught the Dodgers at the end and then beat them in the tense play-off. But then if Sanford and Davenport had not been disabled in 1959, the Dodgers could not have caught the Giants, so these things have a way of balancing out.

They also have a way of helping along heroic deeds. A man on a sixth-place club in the last week of the season has a relaxed air about him. The fans have long ago stopped caring; the pressure is off. He may make a few hits that last week, win a game or two. Who cares?

Over the years there has grown an odd notion that no matter how truly great Willie Mays is, he isn't as great as he ought to be in the clutch. In the last days of the 1962 pennant race and again on the last day of the 1962 World Series, Willie Mays did what he could to lay this ghost to final rest. In the supreme moments of crisis Willie Mays came through. Not just often. *Everytime.*

Keep in mind that the Dodgers led the Giants all through the middle and late stages of the 1962 race. The Giants were a streaky club. The Dodgers would sag, and in San Francisco hope would rise that the Giants would now come on and take advantage of the thinned-out Los Angeles pitching staff. Instead, the Giants would sink to the occasion, surge to the rear with four or five losses in a row. It was a pennant race of reluctant dragons, of Alphonses and Gastons. The line heard most often during the play-offs was that the Yankees were such a cinch to beat either team in the World Series, "it wouldn't go three games."

The Dodgers could not open good ground, even with such cooperation. It was not like 1951, when the Dodgers flew to a thirteen-and-a-half game lead and the Giants played .750 ball to catch up. In 1962, with seven games to go, the Dodgers led by four, a comfortable lead in any other year. In 1965 the Giants led by four with two weeks to go, and it seemed comfortable enough. (It wasn't.) But the same lead, with half the time to blow it—how much safer does a team have to be? Yet Alvin Dark was not conceding. Nor were the Giants. They just weren't able to do anything about it. So the Dodgers did it for them.

On the so-called last day of the season, with the Dodgers leading the league by a game, the Giants entertained Houston up in San Francisco, and the Dodgers played the Cardinals in Los Angeles. Either a Dodger win (unthinkable!) or a Giant loss (thinkable!), and it was all over.

In the eighth inning of a 1-1 game in San Francisco, Willie Mays timed a Dick Farrell fast ball and belted it far over the left-field fence. The Giants won, 2-1. What doubled the pressure was that the Giants full well knew that the Dodgers were also in a tied-up ball game, 0-0. Had the Dodgers led the Cards by five or six runs, no matter what Mays did, it wouldn't have mattered.

Mays responded magnificently. He hit his game-winning home run, and down in Los Angeles Gene Oliver hit a home run off John Podres, and the Dodgers had lost.

In the first inning of the first play-off game, Willie Mays hit another fast ball, this time thrown by a still-ailing Sandy Koufax, and the ball soared into the seats. Later that day, Mays hit a second home run. This was his 49th of the season, to give him leadership in both leagues. He said after the game, "I'll be awful glad when it's over." The strain was showing on Mays. He had fainted in Cincinnati a few weeks earlier and had gone to a local hospital for three days. Exhaustion, the doctors had said. Then the team had gone into a losing spell, and Mays had had to crawl back into uniform to take charge again.

It wasn't until the ninth inning of the play-off decider, the third game, at Dodger Stadium, that Mays made his until-then most important 1962 hit. I was at Dodger Stadium that day, in the temporary press section created for the play-off, when the ninth inning rolled around, the Giants trailing 4-2. I left my seat and wandered below the field to look in at the Giant dressing room. Time had just about run out for San Francisco. Naturally I remembered 1951; you could not escape the analogy. Then the Giants had trailed going into their last at-bats; they had rallied and won. But I also remembered that now Ed Roebuck was giving the Giants fits, that the Giants were more tired and physically ailing than the Dodgers.

When the crowd above the locker rooms made some small pained noises, I took a perch closer to the field than anybody else in the whole park of over 40,000. A park policeman made room for me, and I boosted myself up so that I was more or less lying on the screen, looking down the barrel of the pitching motion, right at the streaking, larger-looming ball and, finally, at two men in scoring position, another man on first, and Roebuck staring at me. I stared back at Roebuck, and in between us was Willie Mays.

Coming down the runway toward the spot I occupied was Dodger traveling secretary Lee Scott. Scott is a dapper little man with a small neat mustache and dark good looks, but beneath his tan you could detect the yellow patina of fear. And as Scott neared the screen—which has a piece of something covering the first five-and-a-half feet, so that you must either be tall or stand on tiptoe or clamber aboard as I had done—Roebuck made his pitch to Mays, Mays whipped his bat around with terrible speed and power, and the sound of the bat meeting the ball was clear and devastating. The ball slashed on a line through the middle of the diamond—a round white rocket.

Scott reached out with one hand and cried out, "What happened, what happened?" He knew too well, but I told him anyway—Roebuck touching the ball, through no willed act of his own—the ball touched him, actually—and dying on the infield grass, and only one run scoring, instead of two, Mays driving in the run that brought the Giants to one run behind, instead of tying it. As I described the play, my eyes swept the stands and saw Dodger fans, their faces white, their hands at their throats or chests. Ask those Dodger fans about Willie Mays.

You can say that Orlando Cepeda's fly ball to right tied the score moments later, that Jim Davenport's walk off Stan Williams put the Giants ahead, that young Possum Burright's error made it a two-run margin, out of reach, but you knew then that Mays had hammered the final nail, slammed the final lid, turned off the lights.

A few minutes later, with Billy Pierce throwing nothing but fast balls, the third out was recorded—a Dodger hitting a soft fly ball to dead centerfield, where Willie Mays tapped his glove three times before putting it away. And with it, the pennant. At the Curran Theatre on San Francisco's Geary Street, where the musical Oliver was playing a matinee, a great cheer rose up from spectators pressing transistor radios to their ears. Mays and the Giants had upstaged Dickens.

We leap now to the fifth game of the World Series, played at Yankee Stadium and won by the Yankees, as they won every odd game, just as the Giants won every even game. The Yankees led the Series, three-two, and I walked into the Giant dressing room, and asked this question to four men: "How would you rate the Giants' chances right now?" I asked Matty Alou, big brother Felipe, Jose Pagan, and Willie Mays.

The two Alous and Pagan used the exact words

and offered nearly the exact same additional comment.

"Our chances are good. Very good." And: "They no beat us in Candlestick."

Mays looked up and made a face that was almost apologetic (because he knew he was supposed to say, "Our chances are good. Remember, we'll be playing at Candlestick.") He spread his hands and said softly, "Who knows? We're down one game."

And so it went, the Giants winning the sixth game, Mays more exhausted than ever, and in the seventh the Yankees taking a razor-edge 1-0 lead when Jack Sanford walked the rival pitcher and a run came home on an anticlimactic double-play ball. Again I walked, late in the game, to the losers' dressing room. Inside I saw Jack Sanford move about the room like a wounded bear, stoop at the water fountain for a sip, turn and pace some more. And listening to a transistor radio someone figured out loud: "If the Giants get a man on in the eighth and a man on in the ninth, and there are no double plays, Mays comes to bat with the tying run on and two out."

It had to be. The year demanded it. The Series confirmed it. Al Silverman of *Sport* magazine said: "If Mays hits a home run in the ninth, he is my man of the year. He gets the car." For years *Sport* has given a spiffy Corvette to the most valuable Series performer. Mays had not had a tremendous Series in the box score: a rash of singles the first day against his "cousin" Whitey Ford and then practically nothing. But he had played centerfield in the Series as though he, and not the Russians, had invented it. Where others were tormented by winds and wet grass (both at Candlestick and the Stadium), where others had let eerie bounces plague them, Mays sauntered, plucked and scooped, an almost unnoticed figure in the field, moving to the fences or to the infield grass, flying right or left, and never appearing to be doing anything other than some completely routine job. Gone was the notion that Mays made hard plays look hard. He may not have had the erect grace of a Joe DiMaggio, but the years had smoothed all his movements into an effortless rhythm. He was, as Stan Musial later called him, "the perfect ballplayer."

Once he had run seventy or eighty feet into right center for a ball and had caught up so easily that he was nearly standing still when he made the catch. You forgot the distance he had travelled getting there. Once he had gone into left center and, as he made a catch, hurdled Felipe Alou, so that Alou slid under him. It was breathless, perfect synchronization. A second time he had gone into left-centerfield, and this time Matty Alou had come over and made the catch, and Mays had slid under Alou. They never touched; they never brushed. The Yankee outfielders played well all Series, but countless times they were banging together, committing last-second lunges, fighting wind, and looking a bit like novices. As did Kuenn, McCovey, and at times Felipe Alou, of the Giants. Only Mays was magnificent in the outfield all Series long.

But Mays had to do it with his bat to win the crowd and the acclaim, and to still (for a moment, anyway) that rap about his ability to hit the ball when it counted. In the final game he tried to drive a ball through the gale that blew in from left field, but the wind held it and pushed it back down, and Tom Tresh made a fine, one-handed catch. Willie McCovey followed with a mighty triple, so who knows, had the wind not been—well.

In the eighth inning a Giant got on, and there was no double play, so in the ninth, it would depend on Matty Alou, Felipe, or Chuck Hiller getting on, for Mays to bat. Pinch-hitter Matty Alou came up, and everybody in the park knew he'd try to drag a bunt. He did, and it got past the pitcher, and Alou was on. We waited. Felipe Alou failed to bunt. (Alou, indomitable, always serious, always trying, had said bitterly in batting practice: "I no heet. No place I can heet. Usually, if the wind blow in from left, it blow out to right, I heet to right. Today—" he shrugged and walked away in gloom.)

Now it was up to Chuck Hiller, and Hiller laid down a marvelous bunt along the third-base line, a bunt that would have been a hit, except that it rolled foul. Then, like Alou, Hiller struck out.

Two out, man on first, Mays up. Later, a reporter said, "You were just trying to hit the ball, weren't you, Willie? Just trying for a base hit?" and Mays looked at him as if the man were crazy and said, "You crazy, man? I was trying for a home run."

Ralph Terry pitched a fast ball, slightly outside. Mays hit it on the nose, but he got no real loft, and the ball sped on a line to right field, headed for the corner. Matty Alou—probably the Giants' fastest runner that day—raced from first around second and headed toward third. He had to stop when Whitey Lockman flagged him.

Later, in a calm, controlled voice, Harvey Kuenn

said: "On any normal day, that ball goes through to the fence. And Alou scores."

But this was the day after six days of rain, and the grass was thick and high and soaking wet. Roger Maris was able to cut off the ball before it reached the fence. From the fence, his throw to Richardson and Richardson's to the plate would have been far too late. And so Mays—in that heart-throbbing moment of climax—had done exactly what he had to do—rifle a base hit toward a far-off fence. Wet grass stymied the logical end, and Willie McCovey, next up, smashed a line drive right at Bobby Richardson. Two feet either way—well, again.

Willie Mays in 1962 hit a few points over .300, led the majors in home runs, was second in the majors in runs batted in, stole bases at a good clip, scored 130 runs, and played a Maysian centerfield. A negative confirmed his greatness and his immense value to his team. The day in September that Mays fainted and was unconscious, they say, some twenty minutes meant the Giants were going to be without their great star for three whole days and parts of two others. The Giants promptly went into a tailspin, and someone went to the record book and discovered this fact: ever since Willie Mays joined the Giants, they had never won a ball game in which he did not make at least a token appearance. With Mays, the Giants have won and lost in roughly a 4-3 ratio. Without Mays—through 1962—the Giants had never won. Nineteen times they had lost.

Chapter Fourteen

The years 1963 and 1964 were like a great breath between the pennant year of 1962 and Mays' gigantic season of 1965. The Giants trailed the pennant-winning Dodgers in 1963 by eleven games, with the Cardinals in between. In 1964 the Giants were down a notch to fourth place, a mere three games behind the Cardinals, who went on to win the World Series, but never actually a likely champion. This was the year the Phillies had won the pennant by September 1 and then collapsed so badly that the team has not been the same since.

So Willie Mays was out of pennant races these two years, and that extra tension, that extra turn of the screw, was missing. Not that Mays did not have his own tensions. As he gets older and his seemingly imperishable skills remain high and polished, we get further glimpses of his utter complexity. Men like Mays are too often taken for granted. Simple and unaffected, yes. But how simple is any man?

While batting on May 8, 1963, Willie Mays suddenly became dizzy and collapsed. The next day he told writer Milton Gross:

"They think I'm made of iron. I want to win as much as anybody, but when you're not up to par, you can't kill yourself. I need the rest but you know I'm not going to ask for it. I feel if the guys I'm playing for, if they don't see it, I'm not going to tell them how tired I am. The first thing they'd say is we're giving you a lot of money."

Yet how much physical fatigue could have been at work here? The date was May 8, the season less than a month old. Mays was thirty-two years old. Had the worry of nearing the time of his career when the road tipped downhill started to gnaw at him? There were indications that it had.

Before the season had started, I saw the Giants play down in San Diego against the Cleveland Indians. Jim Perry pitched for Cleveland against brother Gaylord, and this unimportant game that might have been a friendly contest became an ugly moment of war. Willie McCovey hit a mammoth home run for the Giants in the first inning. Jim Perry's next pitch—to Willie Mays—was a thunderbolt at Mays' head, and Mays was flattened. Cautiously now, Mays got back in. Again Perry flattened him. A couple of innings later, McCovey hit another home run, Mays came up again, and Perry threw a baseball at Mays' left ear. It is the closest I've seen a man come to being killed, without actually being touched, on a ball diamond. Mays got up again, took a toehold, and swung furiously at the next pitch. He missed because he was swinging out of anger, and he was overswinging.

But a pattern had been established, and I do not know whether Jim Perry told National League pitchers, or whether just coincidentally it was decided that

1963 would be a swell year to roll Willie Mays in the dirt. At any rate, this is what happened.

The pitchers let fly and Mays became a target. Oh, he'd been a target for years. But not this way, not so that every game you knew some pitch would come flying in at his ear and send him spinning to the ground. And you never knew when. It might come with men on bases, in a tight spot, or it might come in an early inning. Mays batting with no one on and nothing to gain. The word was out: Shake Mays up; get him on his toes, fidgeting in the box, so he can't dig in.

And Mays knew it. If you saw that TV Special done on Mays by his friend and biographer Charles Einstein, you heard Mays say that no man hits as well after he's been thrown at, *or if he expects to be thrown at again.*

In 1961 Mays had told me that he did not fear such pitchers as Don Drysdale or Stan Williams because they might throw at him. "Shoot," he had said, "I don't worry about throwing at me." Perhaps he didn't really worry about it now; he knew he could get out of the way of any inside pitch; he's always been a most agile man at the plate. But if he was going to see a steady diet of brushback pitching (we're being polite) , he would have to make some accommodations; he'd have to make sure he was ready to bail out.

For the first several weeks in 1963 Mays hit something like .260, or a few points higher as the season moved toward the All-Star break. No wonder, then, that he was in a state of collapse in early May. He wasn't hitting, he was being thrown at every day, he was forced to bat in such a way that he could pull aside from the first errant delivery. Fatigue need not be physical; anxiety is also enervating.

During the early weeks of the 1963 season it didn't look as if he'd pull out of it. But in the All-Star game, Mays got his second wind. He found himself in his element, hitting baseballs thrown by talented pitchers not at his head, but at this corner or that. In fact, Mays had himself one of his typical All-Star days, hitting and running wild, fielding the way he does whether he is bailing out at the plate or not. And the shackles were off: afterwards he was the Willie Mays we know.

By the season's end, he was challenging the league's leading hitters. There he was, the league's sixth leading hitter for average at .314, the league's third home-run hitter, at 38. Once again he scored well over a hundred runs and knocked in over a hundred more. Nobody in the league had hit more extra-base hits than this man who couldn't buy a hit of any size for six weeks. And in the field, the only reason Mays did not go over 400 put-outs in center is that he missed five games. He ended at 397; only Curt Flood, at 403, exceeded Mays in either league.

Baseball is not going to cater to Willie Mays. (Perhaps a little, as Negro prejudice in baseball wears down and out and Negro batters find themselves thrown at no more often than white batters.) Mays is going to be thrown at, steadily, especially now that he had admitted how it disconcerts him. Bench jockeys will not be silent. His personal life will continue to be laid bare not only by newspapermen and magazine writers, but by ballplayers in opposing dugouts. Baseball will not relent. Willie Mays will have to steel himself.

The year 1963 gave us what may be the truest picture yet of Mays. A victim of baseball's wars and of his own doubts for half a season, the rest of the way he was never greater. Flatfooted at the plate, dug in and grim, singleminded, he was a hitting terror. He hit his 38 home runs—to go over the 400 mark—and in one week in August (when he should have been tired), he hit four other baseballs that freakishly struck the top of the centerfield fence at Candlestick Park and fell back onto the field. Instead of four more home runs, Mays had four more doubles. He hit, he ran, he threw. We saw a man who apparently had come to a decision about himself as a ballplayer. He saw no respite, either from the foe or from his own manager and management (and he blasted the Giants, in that quote to Milton Gross after his early collapse, for not recognizing his plight). Except for that one tortured bleat, he stepped out into the war and gave 'em all what for.

He seemed like a man more able to handle his problems, more resigned to his fates. He is aware of the years. On that same TV special, when Charles Einstein said something about getting "slower," Mays said hastily, "Don't use that word," and Einstein made it "less fast." Mays knows he is slower. He knows that he is, as athletes go, aging. He totes all this up to the plate as he digs in against the finest pitchers the National League has seen since the 1930's, when such men as Bill Lee, Dizzy Dean, Lon Warnecke, Carl Hubbell, Paul Derringer, Van Mungo, and Charlie Root were practicing their marvelous art. Baseball has reached a pinnacle of pitching and defense in the National League, and you can count your great hitters by the men today who hit .280 and over, instead of the old-time figure of .300.

In 1964, Mays did not reach that old-time .300. It was the first season since 1956 that he'd fallen below it. As in 1956, Mays hit .296—on any other hitter a swell average. On Mays it did not look good, because early in 1964 he was threatening to hit not .400, but .500. Then came one of his slumps, this one the longest in nearly ten years. In 1956, when Mays dipped below .300, he was 25 years old. In 1964, he was 33. There is a difference; time, it seemed, was short for comebacks. Mays bounced back in 1957, hitting .333. It remained to be seen how much bounce he had left now.

Yet we knew even then that we had to keep a perspective. In this slumping year, Mays still managed to blast out 47 home runs, good enough to lead his league. He batted in 111 runs and scored over 100 runs. He hit doubles and triples at a healthy rate. He suddenly braked a downhill trend in stolen bases. Back in 1956 Mays had stolen 40 bases to lead the league. Ever since, it had been fewer each year, with the exception of 1962, when he stole 18, to match his 18 of the year before. (It took Mays to the first play-off game to get that eighteenth.) In 1963 he stole just eight bases. Surely this looked like age, like a man who was "less fast."

In 1964 he stole 19 bases.

Mays' slump ended just before the season ended. He hit three home runs during the last two days (and three games) against the Cubs, when the Giants had a mathematical possibility of tying for the pennant. And when all is said and done, only four or five men in the sport had put together better years. When Mays became fatigued and sat out a total of three ball games, a New York sportswriter was so incensed he accused Mays of loafing! Mays, who played more games than Clemente, Aaron, Brock, or Frank Robinson!

This is the Mays story: a different set of criteria for Mays than for the rest. Bob Clemente—in 1964—was a better all-around player than Mays, but only because he was four years younger, and because in 1964 Mays had apparently slid downhill. If the slide stopped— say, in 1965—you would have to forget it, because when Mays is right, nobody is better.

And there were moments, even in this 1964 season, that nobody was or could ever have been better. In the first week of September the Giants travelled to Philadelphia to play Gene Mauch's club, merrily on its way to putting a clamp on the pennant. All season long these two teams had battled fiercely. Now the Phils had stretched their lead and the Giants had slumped, what with the business of Al Dark and the racial incident and other morale-sapping events. A most respected and truthful sportswriter, Stan Isaac, had quoted Dark as suggesting that Negroes and Latins were not as mentally alert as white players. Dark, an honest, church-going and tithing gentleman, denied the words attributed to him. Perhaps he had said some of them (this is my interpretation now); perhaps Isaacs had intuitively supplied the rest. In any event, the fat was in the fire and Alvin Dark was, for all intents, through as manager of the Giants. He would go to the next-to-last day and that would be all.

Even with a manager who no longer had the confidence of many of his players, the Giants were obliged to play all out. They came to Philadelphia to do just that. But when the Giants arrived at the Warwick Hotel to open this September three-game set, Willie Mays was not with the team. He had just suffered a fatigue spell in New York. Nobody knew whether he would play in the first of the three games.

Only Gene Mauch knew.

"I don't care *how* tired Willie is," Mauch said. "He'll be out there running and twisting and jumping and hitting. He's never missed a game against the Phillies. Never. One year I told him, 'Willie, you sit out some games against the Phils, and I'll make all your banquet speeches.'"

Mauch was right, of course. There was Mays in uniform the next day. True, he looked desperately tired. But tired or not, he played.

The date was September 4, 1964. There have been better ball games in the history of the National League, but not too many.

In the fourth inning, two out, the Giants leading, 1-0, John Callison punched a single to left field. The Giant pitcher was Dick Estelle, working his first game in the major leagues. Ruben Amaro, who was later traded to the Yankees, was the hitter.

Mays played Amaro the way he plays shallow poke hitters—in so close that he looked like an extra infielder. And Amaro hit probably the longest ball he has ever hit right of center—a curling line smash headed for the scoreboard at the 385-foot mark. Mays whirled and ran. He must have run a hundred feet. He ran as far as he could run and then leaped, left hand extended, his face two feet from the boards. He clutched the ball with that extended gloved hand and threw his legs straight out, so that he wouldn't hit the fence with his face. He hit it with his legs, with a fearful smash. His body seemed to rise, and then he came crashing down on his back.

"For a moment," he said later, "I thought I was hurt. Bad. Then I knew I wasn't." He danced up, flipped the ball to rightfielder Jim Hart, and the stunned Philadelphia crowd, not known for its generosity to a rival player, stood and roared. They roared for five minutes, and then they buzzed for two innings. Later, a few people quibbled. It wasn't the greatest catch they'd ever seen. They could remember one of two others. (Mays had made one a few weeks before in Los Angeles that a few Giants thought was even better.) But most of us in the pressbox and most of the fans and most of the players thought otherwise. It is my own opinion that you cannot make a better play than that one—the run, the catch, the improvised thrusting of legs at the board to break the immediate impact, the daring of the boards, the holding of the ball despite the heavy crash to the ground.

Gene Mauch said with a grin (his team had won): "The only way you can make a better catch is under your armpit."

The next day, Mays did not play. His back had been hurt. He wore a brace, and he sat around. So Mauch had seen a shibboleth destroyed.

The day after, Mays was back. He took extra batting practice, because for one thing he'd missed a day, and for another he'd been in a slump for three months, during which time he'd hit exactly .250. Gene Mauch said aloud, "I don't care if he hits three home runs today, he just isn't swinging right. He's dragging his bat." (Mauch also said ruefully, "I talk too much.")

Dragging the bat, Mays tripled 405 feet off the light tower his first time at bat, and later in the game he taunted Jack Baldschun to throw wildly to first and Frank Thomas to throw wildly to third, and this fatigued ballplayer, his back aching, stole a ball game.

So for all the slumping, this was still a supremely great baseball player. His home-run total was now at 453. Ahead was the Everest, 500. Ahead was 1965.

Chapter Fifteen

At the Fairmont Hotel atop San Francisco's Nob Hill Willie Mays was honored at a $25-a-plate testimonial dinner before the 1965 season got under way. Mays said: I hope I can show my thanks by playing four or five more good years."

Time will tell how many good years are left in Willie Mays. But if he never has a year that comes close to 1965, he will have done enough for baseball and its fans. This was not a "good" year. It was a great year, one of the greatest any player has had in our time. Two men in his league would outhit him for average in 1965—Bob Clemente, with .329, and Hank Aaron, with .318. Mays hit .317. Actually, Aaron hit .3175 and Mays hit .3172, but who's quibbling?

This was Willie Mays' vintage year, the year of his full ripening. There are other years in which he made more hits, stole more bases, and covered more ground, but none in which he was so effortlessly great. Nor, when his injuries made movement itself an effort, had there ever been a year he was so painfully great.

The testimonial at the Fairmont was not the only pre-season banquet for Mays. He received the Paul Shannon Memorial Bowl for "outstanding contribution to baseball" at a dinner of the Boston chapter of

201

the Baseball Writers' Association on January 28, 1965. There were other appearances in Chicago, New York, Rochester, Salt Lake City.

These are the events that tie up a man's time, prevent him from faithfully observing sensible hours and diet, and they involve him in the trivia of travel, speechmaking, and gladhanding. None of this has ever truly appealed to Willie Mays. Yet somehow he seemed to take it all in stride during those early days of 1965.

Then the season opened—in a way Mays has made us accustomed to. He began by belting the ball all over the league.

He had five home runs by May 2. Only Wes Covington had more (six), and Mays soon passed Covington and effortlessly put away other challengers all season long. On May 7, he hit home runs 9 and 10, off Claude Osteen up at Candlestick. The first time Osteen pitched to Mays, he threw a fast ball—his first pitch—and Mays promptly hit it out of sight. The next time Osteen wasted a pitch and then tried his curve; Mays hit this one a little farther. It marked the fifty-first time Mays had hit multiple home runs in a single game. Babe Ruth had 72 such games. And that is how Willie Mays now had to be judged: against Ruth and nobody else. In 1965 you knew he would soon catch whoever was ahead of him in the all-time home run figures.

Mays was hitting so well, so early, that you started to hear the same jokes. A sportswriter wrote: "Mays is off to such a great start, you can expect him to wind up in a hospital earlier than ever."

It didn't happen. At least, not from nerves or fatigue. Mays had his bumps in 1965, many of them very painful. If you dropped into the Giant dressing room from August on, you could always see Mays by himself, in the whirlpool bath, trying to soothe the badly torn muscles. After the whirlpool Mays would lie on the rubbing table, and a Giant trainer would work on him for an hour. Then Mays would take himself into a ball game and make it appear easy.

Not always easy. After he crashed into Philadelphia catcher Pat Corrales right around the All-Star break, Mays limped badly for weeks, and his batting average plummeted. He had been leading the league, but now, in terrible pain, he could barely swing; he could barely run. On top of the groin and hip injuries, he hurt a hand, and now the swing was doubly affected. He could keep just one hand on the bat, so that even when he connected, there was less power than usual.

The muscles finally healed, the hand stopped hurting, and the slumps ended (these were not mental slumps based on anxiety, nervousness, or fatigue; they represented simply a man far from his physical best). You recall what Mays did in August. He took a beaten ball club, hoisted it on his shoulders, and with his bat and his glove carried the team to the top. You know the rest.

Even with the slumps and even without the heroics of August, it was a tremendous season for Mays. He had those early home runs, in clusters, despite his having first strained a groin muscle on May 4. By May 15, he was hitting .389, to lead the league. He hit his fifteenth home run off Larry Jackson in the seventh inning of a May 20 game, to break up a 0-0 game. The Giants won, 2-0. He had numbers 16 and 17 in a doubleheader on May 22, and then he had to rest his various bruises on May 24, which meant the Giants were going to lose, 4-3, to the Braves.

But Mays needs his rest. He said so, for the first time, to his manager in 1965. His manager was Herman Franks, a fat tobacco-chewing man who let it be known from the start that he would rely heavily on Mays, but would also listen to Willie if Willie wanted to rest, or if Willie wanted anything. Before each game, Franks would have Mays in his office for a conference. Mays was the team captain, and it wasn't just a title. (For a while, though, it was a small joke. Vin Scully told how Willie would go to the plate before each game, to go over the ground rules with the umpires and the rival captain or manager, and when he returned to the dugout, his Giant teammates would say, "What did they say, Will?" and Mays would answer, "Everything's in play.") Still, he was the team captain, and an active one. He said just before the season started, "Jay Alou needs to be alternated with his brother. When Jay gets in a slump, all his bad habits come out and he should have a little rest." This is not a profound observation, but it is still a ballplayer suddenly intruding onto a manager's province. In fact, that was exactly what Herman Franks wanted from Mays. His advice. Mays gave it.

He didn't stay at .389, because nobody can any more, not when there are men like Jim Maloney, Seaver, Koosman, Bob Gibson, and Bob Veale around. By the first week in June he was down to .320, going without extra-base hits or runs batted in for some time, but this was because of the first rash of injuries. When they ended, he had seven hits in a double-header on June 20, and pretty soon he was back over .340, leading the league again. On June 23, he hit the 475th home run of his career, off Bob Veale, but a week later he pulled that groin muscle and his average dipped. He was so crippled that he had to play left field, instead of center, and when he added a hip injury to the groin injury after the All-Star break, he again stopped hitting. Franks knew enough to rest him, and Mays had enough confidence in Franks to tell him when he needed rest, so none of the slumps ever developed into one of those painful affairs of the past. Then August came along, the Giants wobbling, and Mays got hot.

The 1965 Giant team was never really much of a ball-club. For all their vaunted power, they were fifth in hitting. They had one superlative pitcher, Juan Marichal, and another reliable pitcher, Bob Shaw, but Shaw had trouble finishing. There were no other consistent starters. In the bullpen, Masanori Murakami and Frank Linzy were far better than expected, but men such as Gaylord Perry and Ron Herbel did less than expected. The fielding was uneasy, too; it had the look of a strong third or fourth-place team.

But no team with Willie Mays is ever truly out of it, especially when Mays is having a year like this. In August he began to hit home runs as though he had invented the blow. That month he hit 17 home runs and batted .363. The incredible began to happen: the Giants began to move up on the Dodgers. On September 6 and 7 the Giants beat the Dodgers twice, to pass Los Angeles by percentage points. Cincinnati was right up there too, and so were Milwaukee and Pittsburgh. But somehow you knew it was the Giants and the Dodgers all over again.

The Giants went into their long winning streak; it reached eleven straight, the Giants in Houston, but then it seemed to have run out. The score was 5-3, Houston, in the top of the ninth inning, with two men out, a man on base, and Willie Mays at the plate. The Houston pitcher was right-hander Claude Raymond—to be exact, Joseph Claude Marc Raymond, a French Canadian. In a situation like this, Mays has no choice. He must try to hit a home run, go for the downs, go for the pump. A base hit does little good, perhaps none. One run does no good.

So Claude Raymond knew that Mays would be dug in, swinging from his heels. Somehow Raymond reacted oddly. You would expect him to throw dinky little curves, snip at the corner, hope to get Mays off balance and have him pop up or hit a ball in the dirt. Instead, Raymond threw fast balls. Nothing but. And as the duel developed, Raymond throwing fast balls, Mays swinging from his heels, it took on a certain epic quality. Perhaps after three or four fast balls Raymond began to think that Mays would have to expect a breaking ball. On this pitch, or *this*, or at least this. Whatever the thinking, they looked like a couple of heavyweights throwing their big punches. On the bench a Giant player breathed: "It's like challenging God."

The count went to 3-and-2—twice Mays had swung

so hard that he had fallen down—and Raymond kept throwing his fast ball. Four times now Mays fouled off 3-and-2 fast balls. Finally, Raymond threw his tenth straight fast ball, and Mays hit it into the left-field seats of the Astrodome, to tie up the ball game. In the tenth inning the Giants won.

On September 28, Mays hit his 51st home run, to tie his all-time Giant mark. It came in Mays' two-thousandth ball game, off a young left-hander named Larry Jaster. Jaster, born in 1944, was seven years old when Willie Mays broke in with the Giants. Now young Jaster—with the Cardinals—beat the Giants, and the Giants fell out of the league lead. They would never regain the lead. And Willie Mays said, "I'd give back that home run any day for a victory. What does a home run mean when we get beat on a night like this?"

Young Jaster also had a word or two. He said he shook inside when he faced the great Giant slugger. He also said, "It's a privilege to pitch against somebody like Mr. Mays."

Finally, on the last day of the season, the pennant over, Willie Mays hit his fifty-second home run, off young Bill McCool of Cincinnati, another youngster who was seven years old when Mays played his first Giant game. The home run came in the fourth inning. It broke the old mark of 51 home runs set by John Mize and Mays himself. Mays trotted from the field shortly after hitting the home run. It was the end of the 1965 campaign.

In the fall of 1965 the votes were counted to determine the National League's Most Valuable Player. Nobody was surprised. Willie Mays had won. In Los Angeles, there was some very mild, low-key grousing. After all, Maury Wills had had a great year. So had Sandy Koufax and Don Drysdale. A Los Angeles reporter asked Drysdale his opinion of the award.

"I think he is very deserving of it," Drysdale said. "It was the greatest year he ever had. I don't see how he could do any more unless he could pitch. The number one reason is he is a natural athlete. He has all the talent in the world and makes the best of it. He is also a great guy, a real competitor on the field, and a real gentleman off the field. I wish he was on our side. He's a pro."

And then Drysdale, a man who has waged some fierce duels with Mays over the years, added the same words young Larry Jaster had used:

"It is a privilege to pitch to him."

Chapter Sixteen

Time passes. Young Larry Jaster is rapidly becoming a veteran. He has played in two World Series; he has moved from the Cardinals to the Montreal Expos, a team that did not exist the day Jaster threw his home-run ball to Willie Mays in the 2000th game of Mays' career. Now Mays has played more than 500 ball games beyond that day and that home run. Don Drysdale, who had competed for so many years against Mays, has retired from baseball in 1969, victim of a sore and aging pitching arm.

Time passes. Baseball once confined itself to the eastern half of the nation. Now it covers the continent from east to west, and reaches into Canada.

Time passes. Mickey Mantle has come and gone. Warren Spahn has retired. So has Roger Maris. Sandy Koufax has thrown his flame for the last time. The 1950s had barely begun when Willie Mays put on his first Giant uniform. Now the 1970s are upon us.

The years are never wholly kind to an athlete. Age takes its toll in strength, speed, reflexes, endurance. The final four seasons of the 1960s, Willie Mays batted under .300 each year. Yet the glory clings, and Mays continued to break records. On May 5, 1966, he belted a Claude Osteen change-up at Candlestick Park, for his 512th career home run, passing Mel Ott as the greatest home-run hitter of his league. A few weeks later he had passed Ted Williams, whom many experts consider to be the greatest slugger since Babe Ruth. With Williams behind, Mays took off after Jimmy Foxx, the brawny strongboy of the Philadelphia Athletics and Boston Red Sox. Foxx, with his tremendous arms, had hammered 534 home runs, some of them among the longest ever hit. On August 16, 1966, Willie Mays looked briefly at a 3-and-2 pitch from righthander Ray Washburn, and then his bat lashed out. The pitch was a slider, waist high, and though Washburn had struck out Mays twice that day, and though Washburn would hurl a no-hit game against Mays and the Giants two years later, this time the bat made contact. The ball flew on a line straight as a telephone wire to clear the right-field fence, 380 feet distant.

With that single swing, Willie Mays had become the second greatest home-run hitter of all time, and the greatest righthanded home-run hitter. It is not simply that writers are plagued with a disease of trivia that we tell you Mays became the premier righthanded home-run hitter. Because baseball employs many more righthanded pitchers, the left handed hitter has a slight advantage. He sees the ball better when it is served up by a righthander; the righthander's curve bends toward his bat and not away. Babe Ruth was lefthanded, and so was Ted Williams and Mel Ott. Mays is righthanded, and so was Foxx, and so is Henry Aaron, closing in on Mays, three years younger than Mays, and with a friendly fence to shoot at. Perhaps some home-run hitters should carry an asterisk after their names, to distinguish the lefthanders from the right.

Right or left, Mays had passed Foxx. The next day a wire arrived: "Congratulations and good luck for the future. I hope that you hit 600." It was signed, Jimmy Foxx. Foxx's own luck would run out before Mays hit number 600. He died, in 1967, choking on a piece of meat.

Number 600 remained elusive for Mays. Going into 1969, Mays had amassed 587 home runs. A few years before, Willie had changed bats, shifting from his old Louisville Slugger model to an Adirondack bat. In appreciation the Adirondack bat people had pledged to give Mays a share of stock for every foot his 600th home run traveled, if and when.

In 1969, Mays suffered more than the usual ills of a competitive ballplayer. His legs began to desert him: knees banged, thigh muscles ripped, feet bruised and aching. Yet the glory still clung. On the second day of the season, Mays stole a base in Atlanta, the three hundredth steal of his career. He is the only ballplayer in history to have stolen 300 or more bases and hit 300 or more home runs. He stole another base the next day. But then he and his legs began to ail. He bruised both knees in a shattering collision at home plate when bringing home the winning run in a game against the Chicago Cubs. He sat out a week of games, came back, reinjured a knee, and sat out ten games. So it went, Mays resting his legs, and then returning to play more of the kind of ball he has always played, tough, sweaty, jarring, sock-it-to-'em. In September, Mays collected his 1190th extra-base hit, to tie Lou Gehrig in this category, and leave just Ruth and Stan Musial ahead. The hit was a triple, driving in two runs, in a game the Giants won, 7-6.

He hurt a leg in running out the triple, and sat out some more games. Back he came, and on September 16 he homered and doubled, to pass Gehrig. More important, the home-run was number 599, and Frank Torre, a former big-league ballplayer and now a representative of the Adirondack Bat company, began to relax. Torre had been following after Mays for weeks, to be on hand for number 600.

On September 22, in San Diego, it happened. Everybody got in on the act. The San Diego Padres, an expansion team that had failed to draw the kind of crowds expansion teams usually draw in their maiden seasons, put on a promotion drive, linked to Mays' impending 600th home run: the fan who would catch the homer in San Diego, would receive a free boxseat for the next season. The promotion was set for September 23 and 24, the last two games Mays and the Giants would play in San Diego. The Padres' management chose to ignore September 22 because it had been reported—and correctly—that Mays would not start that day. His legs were hurting; he was plain exhausted. So only 4779 persons were on hand when in the seventh inning of a tied ball game, Ron Hunt beat out an infield hit, and manager Clyde King waved a hand to Willie Mays, to pinch-hit.

A limping Mays faced rookie Mike Corkins, 22 years old, a righthanded thrower who had faced Willie Mays once before. Mays hadn't remembered, but Corkins had. Mays had hit a home run off Corkins, in spring training. So the youngster knew what he ought not throw to Mays. He gulped, and delivered what he thought he ought.

In the left-field seats, 15-year-old Al Fronlander, Jr. caught the ball, 391 feet from home plate.

Number 600. And 391 shares of Adirondack stock.

For five minutes the fans stood and roared their tribute. Out of the Giant dugout tumbled every player, the manager, the coaches, the trainer, everybody. The dugout emptied. Players met Mays at home plate, pounded him, shouting, hugging, reaching, touching. Fewer than 5000 fans, and mind you, these were enemy fans, yet they sounded like 50,000. Later Mays had to come out of the dugout to doff his cap, so the cheering might subside, and the game continue. But it did not subside. So Mays came out a second time, and finally the crowd stopped roaring.

A handful of men have hit 500 home runs—Ruth, Mays, Foxx, Aaron, Williams, Ott, Mantle, Mathews. But as we move into the 1970s, only Babe Ruth and Willie Mays have hit 600 home runs.

Yet we forget a theme that runs through Willie Mays' career when we isolate the incident, speak only of the home run or the steal or the catch. This 600th home run won a ball game. With the win, the Giants retained a half-game lead over the Atlanta Braves, in the fierce race for the western division of the National League. It would be the last home run Mays would hit in 1969, and it would be the last day the Giants would lead the league. They lost the next night, and Atlanta won: the Giants never caught up. So Mays' feat was again tied to victory, and to a pennant race.

We ignore other themes. As time has passed and Willie Mays has grown older, and the speed, power and reflexes have begun to desert him, other elements of the man demand our attention. More and more Willie Mays' interests overlap the foul lines, and extend beyond the stadium. Some of the interests are those of any healthy pleasure-seeker. Willie Mays plays a solid game of golf, with a 9 handicap. He is among the better scorers in ballplayers golf tournaments. Golf has become an escape and a pleasure for Mays. He has others, too.

One night Mays appeared as a contestant on the television show, The Dating Game, and when the contest was over, you know who won the week in the Bahamas with the shapely young starlet. Yep, Willie Mays. (And you know that Mays spent most of the week playing golf.)

Other moments are more newsworthy. Early in 1967, the California Newspaper Publishers Association gave Mays its annual newsdealer award. Mays had been a newsboy for a brief spell in his youth. Now, of course, he is a newsmaker.

In April of 1968, Mays was named chairman of a drive to raise $2.5-million for the establishment of a health and education center at Miles College, in Birmingham, Alabama, a few miles from his birthplace.

The outside interests do not always exclude baseball. Sometimes the two are inextricably woven. On September 27, 1966, a San Francisco police officer shot and killed a teenage black youngster in the most distressing of the city's black ghettoes, Hunters Point, in the shadow of Candlestick Park. Several hundred youths began to roam the streets of the slum, breaking windows, hurling bricks and gasoline-filled bottles. Over a dozen fires flared. A full-scale riot seemed ready to sweep the city.

That night in Atlanta, nearly 3000 miles away,

Willie Mays belted a home run with two men on, to bring the Giants from a 3-1 deficit to a victory. Willie Mays had driven in 100 runs for the eighth straight year with that blow. Over television and radio, news began to reach the Giants. The next night, September 28, the Giants had another game in Atlanta, and they decided to telecast the game back to San Francisco. Willie Mays hastily made a taped broadcast, to be played on San Francisco radio a hundred times during the day. The idea was to cool the incipient riot by getting young people off the streets and into their homes again.

Said Mays, on the tape: "This is Willie Mays. You know Channel Two is carrying a special program tonight, a game between the Atlanta Braves and the Giants, at six o'clock. I, for one, wish and hope that each and everyone will be tuned in and wishing us well. Of course, I'll be out in center field trying to do my best at all times."

The heat in San Francisco that day reached 95 degrees. Yet people in Hunters Point and elsewhere went back into their teeming apartments and homes, and watched a ball game. The riot died.

Mays' most important interest today is his young son, Michael, adopted three years after he and Marghuerite Chapman had married on Valentine's Day of 1956. Mays is close to his son. He spoke about the boy to reporter Ed Levitt, of the Oakland Tribune: "Mike is very intelligent. I don't want him to be a ball player. I don't want him to go through the kind of aggravation I know he will be up against. They'll start comparing him with me, and that's no good."

If not baseball, then what will the boy do? "One

thing I keep telling him is: 'You're going to finish high school and go on to college.' I don't care if he plays baseball in school. All I care about is ·that he gets an education. My son comes first."

So time passes. Willie Mays, the stickball player, the exuberant child of the streets, has become Willie Mays, the adult, who warns other youths off the street when tragedy might engulf them. Willie Mays, who paid little attention to school as a youngster, knows today the importance of an education for his own son. Time passes. Mays the ballplayer who earned our cheers has become Mays the man who earns our admiration.

Sometimes a single moment fuses Mays the player and Mays the man. Such a moment occurred the day Willie hit that momentous 535th home run, to pass Jimmy Foxx. As Mays concluded his slow stately circle of the bases and neared home plate, Umpire Chris Pelekoudas, behind the plate, broke a century old unwritten rule. He reached out and shook Mays' hand.

Later the umpire would say of this unique tribute:

"We're supposed to be impartial, and I suppose an umpire shouldn't do a thing like that. But when a man reaches baseball immortality, well, I'm not sorry I did it."

Chris Pelekoudas had done what we have all wanted to do for the years and moments of two decades. He simply wanted to say to Willie Mays, Ballplayer and Human:

"Thank you."